# BTEC FIRST

## REVISE BTEC

# Business

Unit 2 Finance for Business

Unit 9 Principles of Marketing

# REVISION GUIDE

North Kent College
The Learning Technology Centre
Tel: 01322 629431

2 1 APR 2016

Oakfield Lane
Dartford
DA1 2JT

Series Consultant: Harry Smith

Authors: Carol Carysforth and Mike Neild

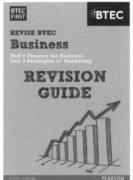

## THE REVISE BTEC SERIES

This Revision Guide is designed to complement your classroom
and home learning, and to help prepare you for the exam.
It does not include all the content and skills needed for the
complete course. It is designed to work in combination
with Pearson's main BTEC First series.

**To find out more visit:**
www.pearsonschools.co.uk/revise

NWKC

072518

ALWAYS LEARNING

**PEARSON**

Published by Pearson Education Limited, Edinburgh Gate, Harlow, Essex, CM20 2JE.

www.pearsonschoolsandfecolleges.co.uk

Copies of official specifications for all Pearson qualifications may be found on the website: www.edexcel.com

Text © Pearson Education Limited 2014
Typeset by Tech-Set Ltd, Gateshead
Original illustrations © Pearson Education Limited
Cover photo/illustration by Miriam Sturdee

The rights of Carol Carysforth and Mike Neild to be identified as authors of this work has been asserted by them in accordance with the Copyright, Designs and Patents Act 1988.

First published 2014

17 16 15 14
10 9 8 7 6 5 4 3 2 1

**British Library Cataloguing in Publication Data**
A catalogue record for this book is available from the British Library

ISBN 978 1 4469 0668 2

**Copyright notice**
All rights reserved. No part of this publication may be reproduced in any form or by any means (including photocopying or storing it in any medium by electronic means and whether or not transiently or incidentally to some other use of this publication) without the written permission of the copyright owner, except in accordance with the provisions of the Copyright, Designs and Patents Act 1988 or under the terms of a licence issued by the Copyright Licensing Agency, Saffron House, 6–10 Kirby Street, London EC1N 8TS (www.cla.co.uk). Applications for the copyright owner's written permission should be addressed to the publisher.

Printed in Slovakia by Neografia

**Acknowledgements**
The publisher would like to thank the following for their kind permission to reproduce their photographs:
(Key: b-bottom; c-centre; l-left; r-right; t-top)

**Alamy Images:** Danny Callcut 51l, david pearson 61cr, dpa picture alliance 42r, Gregory Wrona 49cl, Image Source 26tl, Kevin Wheal 55cr, Steve Morgan 58cl; **Corbis:** Splash News 59cl; **Courtesy of Samsung:** 54tl (Bottomleft), 54tl (BottomRight), 54tl (Top); **Courtesy of Trunki:** 46tr; **Deutsche Post DHL:** 43l; **DK Images:** Ian O'Leary 2b; **Facebook.com:** 60tl; **Fotolia.com:** Adam Borkowski 12cr, Africa Studio 42l, Alliance 17bl, alma_sacra 21cr, Andres Rodriguez 41r, apops 1tr, bloomua 63br, Chepko Danil 2tr, Creativa 53c, Faysal Farhan 60cl, govicinity 17cl, 23tl, happystock 5tl, imtmphoto 40cr, jamdesign 62tr, Maksim Shebeko 21br, monjiro 64cl, Monkey Business 19br, 28b, Patryk Kosmider 52tl, Picture-Factory 8c, rgbdigital.co.uk 55cl, Varina Patel 7tr, Viktorija 24br; **Getty Images:** Eamonn M.McCormack 60cr, George Doyle 2tl, Nicole S. Young 48, Sparky / The Image Bank 45tl; **Go Ape Tree Top Adventure (www.goape.co.uk):** 44cl; **Pearson Education Ltd:** Gareth Boden 13br, Rob Judges 39tr; **Rex Features:** Geoff Wilkinson 49; **Shutterstock.com:** 0833379753 26bl, Adriano Castelli 39tl, Blend Images 1br, SimonHS 8tr; **Twitter, Inc:** 60tr; **Veer / Corbis:** Andresr 7bl, Artur Marciniec 52tr, Darren Kemper 24t, Devon Yu 11, homestudio 33cl, _human 4b, ia_64 3tr, jirkaejc 44cr, Kzenon 62tl, Maxx-Studio 25bl, 29cr, Monkey Business Images 4tr, 6tl, nito 18tr, onepony 56tr, Peter Guess 17cr, Piccia Neri 61cl, Plus69 5tr, rbouwman 45tr, RuthBlack 27bl, TAlex 51r, Timmary 41l, tuja66 22cr, veerguy 56tc, wavebreakmediamicro 14cr, 46tl, Zidi 40cl
All other images © Pearson Education

**Picture Research by:** Susie Prescott

Every effort has been made to trace the copyright holders and we apologise in advance for any unintentional omissions. We would be pleased to insert the appropriate acknowledgement in any subsequent edition of this publication.

---

**A note from the publisher**

In order to ensure that this resource offers high-quality support for the associated BTEC qualification, it has been through a review process by the awarding body to confirm that it fully covers the teaching and learning content of the specification or part of a specification at which it is aimed, and demonstrates an appropriate balance between the development of subject skills, knowledge and understanding, in addition to preparation for assessment.

While the publishers have made every attempt to ensure that advice on the qualification and its assessment is accurate, the official specification and associated assessment guidance materials are the only authoritative source of information and should always be referred to for definitive guidance.

BTEC examiners have not contributed to any sections in this resource relevant to examination papers for which they have responsibility.

No material from an endorsed book will be used verbatim in any assessment set by BTEC.

Endorsement of a book does not mean that the book is required to achieve this BTEC qualification, nor does it mean that it is the only suitable material available to support the qualification, and any resource lists produced by the awarding body shall include this and other appropriate resources.

# Contents

This book covers the externally assessed units in the BTEC Level I/Level 2 First in Business qualification.

- - - - - - - - - - - - - - - - - - - - - -

## A small bit of small print

Pearson publishes Sample Assessment Material and the Specification on its website. That is the official content, and this book should be used in conjunction with it. The questions in the *Now try this* sections have been written to help you practise every topic in the book. Remember: the real test questions may not look like this.

1-to-1 page match with the BTEC First in Business Revision Workbook ISBN 978-1-446-90669-9

# Start-up costs

COSTS are the money paid out by a business for the items it needs. Before a business can begin TRADING, it usually needs to spend money. These expenses are called START-UP COSTS.

## Start-up costs for Sam's Sandwiches

Here are TWO examples of start-up costs that a new sandwich shop might have.

1

Buying and installing a sign.

2

Paying for a cash register.

## Worked example

Jason is starting a gardening business. He and an assistant will travel to customers' houses and mow their lawns and look after their gardens.

> Give **two** examples of start-up costs Jason might have.   **(2 marks)**

**1**

| Buying a lawnmower |

**2**

| Buying a van |

Think of things Jason will need **before** he starts work. Be careful that you do not include **on-going** costs like paying wages or buying fertiliser. There is more about costs like these on page 2.

## Paying for start-up costs

Businesses must pay their start-up costs BEFORE they start trading. This means that money for start-up costs must be raised from SAVINGS or from LOANS.

## Online test

Remember that your Unit 2 exam will be ONLINE. Read the question carefully before you answer it. Sometimes you might have to click an image or move a tile. If you type an answer in a box, use good spelling, and make sure your answer is SPECIFIC to the context of the question.

## Now try this

Sarah is going into business making celebration cakes. She wants to convert her garage into a commercial kitchen.

> Give **two** examples of start-up costs Sarah might have.   **(2 marks)**

Make sure your response is specific to Sarah's business.

# Operating (running) costs

OPERATING (RUNNING) COSTS are the EXPENSES a business has in its day-to-day operations.

## Running costs for Sam's Sandwiches

Here are TWO examples of running costs that the sandwich shop might have.

**1** Ingredients and staff wages are running costs for a sandwich shop.

**2** Utility bills for water, gas and electricity are running costs. So, too, are rent and rates.

## Operating costs

Running costs are sometimes called OPERATING COSTS because they are the costs involved in operating the business.

Running costs usually occur AGAIN AND AGAIN.

### Running costs or start-up costs?

In the online test you may have to identify which costs are running costs and which costs are start-up costs.

Start-up costs only occur before the business opens.

## Worked example

Some of the costs for Jason's gardening business are shown below. Tick the box to show whether each statement is a start-up cost or a running cost.

> Which of these are start-up costs and which are running costs? **(4 marks)**

Both the lawnmower and van are needed **before** Jason can start work, so they must be **start-up costs**. Paying wages and buying diesel will happen again and again so these are **running costs**.

| | Start-up costs | Running costs |
|---|---|---|
| Buying a lawnmower | ✓ | ☐ |
| Purchasing a van | ✓ | ☐ |
| Paying wages to an assistant | ☐ | ✓ |
| Buying diesel for the van | ☐ | ✓ |

In the online test you may be asked to select the correct items from a list. You won't be able to select **all** the boxes, and you can **change** your answer as often as you like before finishing.

## Now try this

Sarah makes celebration cakes.

> Give **two** examples of running costs she might have. **(2 marks)**

Make sure your answer is specific to Sarah's business. Think about what Sarah would have to spend money on as part of the **day-to-day** running of her business.

# Fixed and variable costs

The RUNNING COSTS of a business can be divided into FIXED COSTS and VARIABLE COSTS. Businesses also have DIRECT and INDIRECT costs. Fixed costs are often indirect and variable costs are often direct.

## Fixed and variable costs

Fixed costs STAY THE SAME no matter how many products the business makes or sells.

Wendy has to pay £30 for a pitch no matter how many hot dogs she sells. This is an example of a FIXED COST.

Variable costs CHANGE depending on the number of products made or sold.

The more hot dogs Wendy sells, the more rolls and sausages she needs. This is an example of a VARIABLE COST.

## Direct and indirect costs

A DIRECT COST is directly related to output, for example the cost of wood in a furniture factory. An INDIRECT COST is independent of output, for example the cost of staff uniforms.

The ingredients used to make Wendy's hot dogs are a **variable cost**.

---

## Worked example

Anna makes silver jewellery in her garage and sells it online.

> **1** Give **one** example of a fixed cost that Anna might have.                    **(1 mark)**

Internet access

> **2** Give **one** example of a variable cost that Anna might have.                    **(1 mark)**

Cost of materials

Think about the costs that Anna has, no matter how much jewellery she sells. Other examples of **fixed costs** might be:
• rent
• utility bills
• insurance.

Think about the costs that increase as Anna sells more jewellery. Other examples of **variable costs** might be:
• postage and packing
• commissions paid to a website
• credit card fees.

---

## Now try this

In his workshop, Ken makes wooden rocking horses for small children and paints them in bright colours. He usually makes ten horses each week.

> **(a)** Give **one** example of a fixed cost Ken's business might have.                    **(1 mark)**
>
> **(b)** Give **one** example of a variable cost Ken's business might have.                    **(1 mark)**

# Calculating total costs

You might need to calculate costs for a business. You can use the FIXED COSTS and the VARIABLE COSTS to calculate the TOTAL COSTS. You need to learn how to calculate total costs.

## Calculating total costs

TOTAL COSTS are ALL the costs of a business.

| WENDY'S HOT DOGS | |
| --- | --- |
| Fixed costs | £30 |
| Variable costs | +£40 |
| Total costs | £70 |

They are calculated using this formula:

$$\text{TOTAL COSTS} = \text{FIXED COSTS} + \text{VARIABLE COSTS}$$

## Calculating variable costs

Variable costs change depending on the number of UNITS produced or sold. It may be useful for you to know the formula:

$$\text{VARIABLE COSTS} = \text{COST OF ONE UNIT} \times \text{NUMBER OF UNITS}$$

Number of hot dogs sold = 200
Cost per hot dog = 20p

Variable cost = 20p × 200
= 4000p
= £40

## Worked example

Jenny plans to start making bracelets to sell. She has estimated the following monthly costs if she sells 40 bracelets:
- variable costs of £15 for each bracelet she sells
- fixed costs of £300.

**1** Complete the table using this information. **(2 marks)**

|  | 40 items sold |
| --- | --- |
| Variable costs | £600 |
| Fixed costs | £300 |
| Total costs | £900 |

£15 × 40
= £600

**2** What would be the total cost if Jenny sold 50 items? **(2 marks)**

£1,050

Make sure you have a calculator nearby when you are practising questions like these.

## Calculator tool

In your online test you can use the calculator tool to work out calculations like the ones above.

## Now try this

James runs a business making wicker chairs. He estimates the following monthly costs:
- variable costs of £30 for each chair he makes
- fixed costs of £120.

James makes six chairs in February.

**1** Work out James' variable costs for February. **(1 mark)**

**2** Work out James' total costs for February. **(1 mark)**

Use both the formulae in this question:

$$\text{Variable costs} = \text{Cost of one unit} \times \text{Number of units}$$

$$\text{Total costs} = \text{Fixed costs} + \text{Variable costs}$$

You need to learn these formulae. They will not be given to you in the online test.

# Sources of revenue

REVENUE is money received by a business. Most revenue comes from SELLING PRODUCTS and SERVICES.

## Revenue for Jim's Computer Shop

Here are TWO examples of sources of revenue that a computer shop might have.

 The SALE of equipment and consumables (for example, printer cartridges) is one source of revenue.

 REPAIRING faulty equipment is another source of revenue.

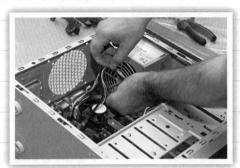

## Other sources of revenue

Jim rents out the rooms upstairs he never uses. He puts this money into a savings account.

Jim now has two more sources of revenue:

 RENT.

 INTEREST.

Businesses try to identify additional sources of revenue to earn as much money as possible.

Jim could create two more sources of revenue by:

 Charging extra for visiting clients to repair their computers.

 Offering maintenance contracts to businesses.

## Worked example

Sam, Louise and Sharmeen are vets. They run a local practice specialising in small animal care.

> Give **two** sources of revenue their practice might have. **(2 marks)**

1  `Charging for consultations`

2  `Selling pet products`

Think about other ways the practice will make money, such as:
- selling pet food
- charging for annual vaccinations
- charging for pet medicines.

## Now try this

> Which **two** of the following are sources of revenue for a charity shop? **(2 marks)**

A ☐ Advertising the shop    B ☐ Selling clothes

C ☐ Donations from the public    D ☐ Collecting items to sell

E ☐ Paying rent for the shop

In the test remember to think carefully about the particular type of business and how it can earn money.

# Calculating revenue

REVENUE is the money a business receives. You might need to calculate the REVENUE for a business.

## Using a formula

You must LEARN and REMEMBER this formula for calculating revenue for your online test.

$$\text{REVENUE} = \frac{\text{NUMBER}}{\text{OF SALES}} \times \frac{\text{PRICE}}{\text{PER UNIT}}$$

At the village fete Wendy sold 200 hot dogs at 70p.

Number of hot dogs sold = 200
Price of each hot dog = 70p
Revenue received = 200 × 0.70
            = £140

## Total revenue

Many businesses sell more than one product or service.

In this case you would calculate the revenue for each product and then add them together to get the TOTAL REVENUE.

## Calculating total revenue

Wendy also sold 250 burgers at £1.50 each.

Village Fete:
Pitches
£30 a day.

Wendy's
Hot dogs
and Burgers

Number of burgers sold = 250
Price of each burger = £1.50
Revenue received = 250 × £1.50 = £375

**WENDY'S TOTAL REVENUE**

| | |
|---|---|
| Revenue from hot dogs | £140 |
| Revenue from burgers | +£375 |
| Total revenue | £515 |

Revenue always means the money a business receives.

Wendy used the formula to calculate her revenue from selling hot dogs and burgers. Then she added these two figures together.

## Worked example

A small business sells personalised T-shirts. Each one retails for £15. The business sold 10,000 T-shirts last year.

Calculate the revenue for the business.   **(2 marks)**

Revenue = 10,000 × £15 = £150,000

£150,000

In the online test, use the calculator tool to work out the answer and the box for workings to show your calculations.

Remember to include the working out in your answer! In the test you will have a box just for your working.

## Now try this

Last week a charity shop held a book and DVD fair. It sold 1,200 books at 25p each and 500 DVDs at 20p each.

Calculate the **total revenue** it earned.   **(3 marks)**

Do this task step by step:
1 Calculate revenue for the books.
2 Calculate revenue for the DVDs.
3 Add your answers together.

# Types of expenditure

EXPENDITURE is money the business pays out. Everyday RUNNING COSTS are called OVERHEADS.

## Overheads at Tilly's Sweet Shop

Tilly has a sweet shop. Examples of overheads that Tilly must pay are:

- wages for her assistant
- rent
- business rates
- utility bills (for electricity, gas and water).

## Other types of expenditure

- Tilly must buy stock to sell.
- She might also spend money on advertising or have a website so that she can sell sweets online.
- If Tilly sells sweets online then she will also need to pay for an internet connection and may need to pay to build a website, as well as postage and packing charges.

## Remember the difference

- STOCK is bought by retailers for resale (e.g. Tilly's sweets).
- CONSUMABLES are used by the business itself (e.g. paper for till receipts).
- RAW MATERIALS are used by manufacturers to make a product (e.g. sweet manufacturers need sugar).

## Calculating expenditure

On page 4, you calculated total costs.

All businesses must calculate and record how much they spend. They need this information to work out if they have made a PROFIT or a LOSS.

## Worked example

Jake is a greengrocer.

> Which **two** of these are items of expenditure for a greengrocer? **(2 marks)**

A ☑ Stock for the shop

B ☐ A bank loan for an extension

C ☑ Wages for his assistant

D ☐ Sales revenue

E ☐ Interest on savings in the bank

Expenditure is the opposite of revenue. Expenditure always means money a business pays out.

## Spending to succeed

Every business must spend money in order to make money. Tilly may spend money on advertising to build awareness of her business. Money might be spent on improving the look of the store to attract passing trade.

## Now try this

Always make sure you read the question carefully. This question needs you to identify **two** figures.

Lucy runs a nail bar.

> Which **two** figures show her expenditure items this month? **(2 marks)**

A ☐ Rent £1,000

B ☐ Product sales £200

C ☐ Income from manicures £2,600

D ☐ Wages £1,400

# Understanding and calculating profit or loss

All businesses want to make a PROFIT. This happens when REVENUE is MORE THAN EXPENDITURE.

## Making a profit

Making a profit means the business can grow. The owner can buy new equipment or open another outlet.

### Calculating profit

You calculate profit using the following formula:

PROFIT = REVENUE − EXPENDITURE

> You must learn the formula for profit so that you can use it in the online test.

## Making a loss

Sometimes a business makes a loss. This happens when EXPENDITURE is MORE THAN REVENUE.

Businesses that make losses often have to stop trading.

---

## Worked example

Gary is a window cleaner. Last year his revenue was £40,000 and his expenditure was £10,000.

> Did he make a profit or a loss? **(1 mark)**

Show how you calculated your answer.

| | |
|---|---|
| Revenue | £40,000 |
| Expenditure | −£10,000 |
| Profit | £30,000 |

Gary made a profit.

> Gary's revenue was greater than his expenditure so he made a **profit** of £30,000.

## Increasing profits

Businesses try to INCREASE their profits by:

* increasing their revenue, and/or
* reducing their expenditure.

In year 2, Gary gains more customers so he earns more money. He also spends less on advertising. Now his revenue is £45,000 and his expenditure is £9,000.

He does the following calculation:
Profit = £45,000 − £9,000
= £36,000

Gary's profits have INCREASED by £6,000.

---

## Now try this

> Give the formula to calculate profit by selecting the correct words from the box. **(1 mark)**

| | | |
|---|---|---|
| Running costs | Overheads | Expenditure |
| Loss | Variable costs | Revenue |

Profit = [_____] − [_____] .

> In the online test you may have to show you can remember the formula by identifying the right words from several options.

# Break-even charts

BREAKEVEN is when revenue and expenditure (costs) are the SAME. There is no profit and no loss because the money that the business has made through selling a product is equal to the cost of making the product.

## Break-even charts

A BREAK-EVEN CHART can be drawn to show how much a business needs to sell to BREAK EVEN and how much it will need to make to start making a profit.

### Online test

In the online test you may be asked to identify specific areas on a chart, such as the break-even point.

---

LOSS is shown by the space between costs and revenue BELOW the break-even point.

PROFIT is shown by the space between costs and revenue ABOVE the break-even point.

VARIABLE COSTS e.g. raw materials, change as output increases.

TOTAL REVENUE starts at zero as no sales means no income. It increases directly with the number of items sold.

The BREAK-EVEN POINT is where the total cost and revenue lines cross. This is shown as an X on the chart.

TOTAL COSTS shows the fixed costs plus variable costs.

When the TOTAL REVENUE line is higher than the TOTAL COSTS line, the business makes a PROFIT. When it is not, it makes a LOSS.

MARGIN OF SAFETY is the amount by which sales would have to fall before the break-even point is reached.

FIXED COSTS e.g. rent are shown by a horizontal line because these do not change with output.

*(Chart axes labelled: Costs and revenue (£) on vertical axis, Units on horizontal axis)*

---

## Worked example

Jacqui has a new business and is drawing a break-even chart.

**1** Define the term 'break-even point'. **(1 mark)**

Make sure you give a clear and accurate definition for a term.

When a business has made enough money through product sales to cover the cost of making the product.

### Now try this

**2** Give **two** items of information Jacqui needs to know before she can start to create her break-even chart. **(2 marks)**

Her fixed costs and her variable costs.

She also needs to know the price she intends to charge, so that she can calculate her predicted revenue.

Complete each sentence below. **(2 marks)**

**A** The total costs line on a break-even chart represents fixed costs + _____ .

**B** Where the total costs line crosses the total revenue line, this shows _____ .

# Interpreting break-even charts

Break-even charts provide lots of financial information about businesses so it's important to be able to interpret them.

## Understanding the information shown on a break-even chart

- The VERTICAL AXIS on a break-even chart shows MONEY, i.e. costs and revenue.
- The HORIZONTAL AXIS on the chart shows UNITS, i.e. the number of items produced.
- The BREAK-EVEN POINT is the point where the total costs and revenue lines cross.

Reading off the numbers that are shown by the lines gives vital information, such as the:

- FIXED COSTS of the business
- TOTAL COSTS at every level of sales
- VARIABLE COSTS at every level of sales (i.e. the total costs MINUS the fixed costs)
- TOTAL REVENUE at every level of sales
- NUMBER OF UNITS that must be sold to break even
- PROFIT or LOSS that can be made
- MARGIN OF SAFETY planned by the business.

## Worked example

Dev makes wooden toy boxes. Here is a break-even chart for his business.

**1** What are the **fixed costs** for Dev's business? **(1 mark)**

£4,000

**2** What are his **total costs** if he sells 200 toy boxes? **(1 mark)**

£12,000

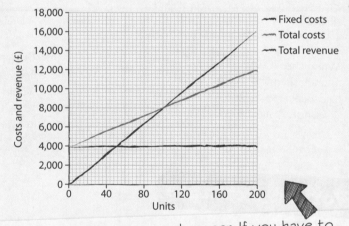

The chart in the online test is shown on graph paper. If you have to read off a number, use a ruler or trace the horizontal or vertical line carefully with your finger to make sure you read it accurately.

You may also be asked to present information graphically on a prepared break-even chart. This could be identifying the break-even point or other areas, such as profit or loss.

## Now try this

Dev is using his break-even chart from the worked example to plan his first year of business. Help him by providing the following information.

**1** Identify the number of toy boxes Dev must make to **break even**. **(1 mark)**

Dev thinks he could sell up to 200 toy boxes.

**2** What is his **total revenue** if he does? **(1 mark)**

**3** What is the **selling price** of Dev's toy boxes? **(1 mark)**

Find the selling price by dividing Dev's total revenue by the maximum number of toy boxes he could sell.

# Using the breakeven formula to calculate the break-even point

Another way to calculate the BREAK-EVEN POINT is to use the BREAKEVEN FORMULA.

## Breakeven formula

The formula for calculating breakeven is:

$$\text{Breakeven} = \frac{\text{Fixed costs}}{\text{Selling price per unit} - \text{Variable cost per unit}}$$

Stacey valets each car for £35. Her variable costs are £5 per car and her fixed costs are £300 a month. Her break-even calculation would be:

$$\frac{£300}{£35 - £5} = \frac{£300}{£30} = 10$$

She would have to valet 10 cars a month to break even.

### Don't worry

You do NOT need to learn the formula for breakeven. If you need it in the online test, it will be given to you.

You will also be given the data you need.

### Changing the selling price

Using the formula can show you quickly what would happen if you changed the selling price.
- If you INCREASE the price then your break-even point falls.
- If you REDUCE the price, it becomes higher.

## Worked example

Kamaljit makes silver bracelets. She has recorded her predicted figures for next year in a table.

| How many bracelets would she need to sell to **break even**? | **(1 mark)** |

90

|  | £ |
|---|---|
| Selling price per bracelet | 80 |
| Variable cost per bracelet | 20 |
| Fixed costs | 5,400 |

In the online test, put the figures into the working box and use the calculator function.

$$\text{Breakeven} = \frac{5,400}{80 - 20}$$
$$= \frac{5,400}{60}$$
$$= 90$$

## Now try this

A business makes mountain bikes. This table shows its predicted figures for next year.

|  | £ |
|---|---|
| Selling price per bike | 300 |
| Variable cost per bike | 150 |
| Fixed costs | 60,000 |

**1** How many bikes would the business need to sell to **break even**? **(1 mark)**

**2** If the selling price increased to £350 per bike and the costs remained the same, what would be the new break-even point? **(1 mark)**

**3** If the selling price was reduced to £250 per bike and the costs remained the same, what would be the new break-even point? **(1 mark)**

# The value of breakeven analysis and the risks of ignoring it

BREAKEVEN ANALYSIS is a planning tool that helps businesses to make the right decisions and increase their chance of success.

## The benefits of breakeven analysis

- ✓ The business knows the FIXED and VARIABLE costs linked to a product.
- ✓ The business can analyse costs to see if any are too high and can be REDUCED.
- ✓ The business can set the OPTIMUM (BEST) PRICE for a product.
- ✓ The business can CALCULATE and FORECAST potential sales REVENUE.
- ✓ It allows the business to stock or make the most PROFITABLE GOODS.
- ✓ It allows the business to set a MARGIN OF SAFETY.

## The risks of ignoring breakeven analysis

- ✗ The business does NOT know the costs of production and RUNNING costs.
- ✗ The cost of stock or raw materials may be too high.
- ✗ The selling price may be too high, too low or not cover costs.
- ✗ The business does not know how many items it must sell to make a PROFIT.
- ✗ The business may make a LOSS without realising or knowing why.
- ✗ The MARGIN OF SAFETY is unknown.

## Breakeven analysis is used:

- when a new business is being set up
- when a new product is being launched
- to set realistic production targets
- to set realistic sales targets
- to review and analyse past performance.

Breakeven analysis also lets you analyse the effect on the break-even point if costs change (see page 13).

The benefits and risks are easier to remember if you think of them as opposites. Try reading them in pairs across the page.

Ensuring you set realistic production targets will help your business in the long run.

## Worked example

Ben wants to make and sell surfboards.

Which **two** of these are benefits of carrying out breakeven analysis before he starts?          **(2 marks)**

A ✓ He knows his costs

B ☐ He has identified his customers

C ☐ His sales are guaranteed

D ✓ He can set the sales price to cover costs

E ☐ He doesn't know his margin of safety

If you are asked to discuss the use of breakeven analysis, this means explaining the actions Salma should take, what information she should obtain and how this information could affect her business decision.

## Now try this

Salma has a good idea for an app but would have to pay to get it developed.

Discuss the use of breakeven analysis in helping her to plan for a successful business.
          **(8 marks)**

To gain eight marks, you should give an in-depth explanation of how breakeven analysis can be used to make Salma's business successful.

# The effect of changes on the break-even point

The break-even point will change if total costs change or if the selling price changes. Both can have an impact on the business.

## Rising costs

A rise in fixed or variable costs increases TOTAL COSTS. More items must now be sold to break even. An increase in costs always means the break-even point rises too.

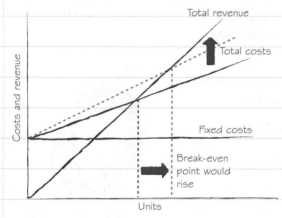

If costs rise, the business could:
- try to reduce these costs (change suppliers, use cheaper raw materials, etc.)
- increase the selling price to try to get more revenue.

Both actions would LOWER the break-even point and help to increase profits.

**Caution!** Businesses must be careful about increasing the selling price because customers may switch to a cheaper alternative and sales would then fall.

## Falling costs

If costs FALL, the break-even point is LOWER so the business makes more profit.

The LOWER the break-even point, the FEWER the sales needed to make a profit.

## Falling sales

A business can try to improve falling sales by lowering the selling price. However, this INCREASES the number of goods that need to be sold to break even, as you saw on page 11.

A business may lower the price for a short time only, to help boost sales and attract new customers.

## Worked example

Sophia has a shop. Her rent has increased and she is concerned about how this will affect her business.

**1** Describe the effect of this increase on her break-even point and the business. **(2 marks)**

> Her break-even point will rise. She must sell more to break even.

**2** Explain **one** action she could take to help the business. **(2 marks)**

> She could try to reduce her other costs as this will lower her break-even point.

The box provided for a written answer in the online test will scroll down, so you will never run out of space.

## Now try this

Sally and Brian run a restaurant. Their gas bills have increased at a time when the business is only just breaking even.

**1** Describe **one** impact of this on their business. **(2 marks)**

Sally suggests promoting a special menu that has higher prices for dishes made with local ingredients.

**2** How will this affect their break-even point? **(1 mark)**

**3** Identify **one** risk associated with Sally's idea. **(1 mark)**

# The purpose of budgeting

The purpose of BUDGETING is to keep expenditure to a planned limit, because if expenditure is less than revenue, the business will make a profit.

## Revenue budgets

The budget identifies SALES TARGETS and therefore REVENUE.

$$\text{Total SALES REVENUE} = \text{Number of sales} \times \text{Price per unit}$$

Sales revenue is vital for profits so businesses often set high sales targets for their staff.

## Expenditure budgets

The budget also sets SPENDING TARGETS.

The agreed target is the total amount of allowable EXPENDITURE (for example, wages, overheads, raw materials).

To make a profit, revenue must be HIGHER than expenditure.

## A financial planning tool

Budgeting is another financial planning tool that helps businesses to plan for success by:
- setting sales targets
- identifying and limiting expenditure.

An established business will use last year's revenue and expenditure figures as a basis.

A new business will have to list all its possible items of expenditure.

## Coping with emergencies

All businesses may have unexpected items of expenditure, such as a car repair. To cope with this, some money may be set aside as a cushion or CONTINGENCY FUND.

This fund should only be used if there is an emergency.

---

## Worked example

Hamida has prepared her first budget.

Budget:  Forecast sales revenue  £30,000
Forecast expenditure  £10,000

Profit = Revenue − Expenditure.
The higher the revenue and the lower the expenditure, the greater the profit.

**1** If Hamida keeps to her budget, how much profit will she make?  **(1 mark)**

£20,000

**2** If Hamida's expenditure increases by £5,000, how will this affect her profit?  **(1 mark)**

It will fall to £15,000

---

## Now try this

Kim is planning on starting a new business.

Explain **one** benefit to Kim of preparing a budget.

**(2 marks)**

Write an explanation by identifying a benefit and saying how it will help Kim's business.

# Budgeting and budgetary control

BUDGETING means setting a budget. BUDGETARY CONTROL means checking performance to make sure that targets are met and are within budget.

## Setting the budget

Setting a budget involves setting and agreeing:
- SALES REVENUE TARGETS
- EXPENDITURE LIMITS.

The aim is to MAKE A PROFIT.

## Controlling the budget

| Checking SALES LEVELS (usually monthly) | → | Checking SPENDING (usually monthly) | → | TAKING PROMPT ACTION if sales are too low or spending is too high |

The aim is to KEEP THE BUDGET ON TRACK.

## Checking spending

Actual spending must be compared regularly with predicted spending.
- Rising costs should be reduced, if possible.
- If there is regular overspending on certain items, this must be investigated.

## Worked example

Hamida has set her first budget.

**1** What action should she now take to control the budget? **(1 mark)**

> Hamida should check each month that she is meeting her planned revenue and expenditure targets. This is called budgetary control.

**2** Last month she had to spend an extra £50 on insurance. How will this affect her budget? **(1 mark)**

> This will mean she will overspend and not meet the targets she had set.

## Checking sales levels

Actual revenue must be compared with predicted revenue.
- Action must be taken to boost sales if they are too low.
- Ideally, this should be done WITHOUT spending more money.

The sales and spending levels in a budget must be:
- achievable
- appropriate
- realistic.

They may need revising if they are too ambitious.

## Now try this

Sye has set his budget but has not checked it recently.

Explain **one** reason budgetary control is important to his business. **(2 marks)**

1 Start your answer by giving one thing that budgetary control can do.
2 Then explain what could happen to Sye's business if the thing you identified doesn't take place.

# Cash flow forecasting

CASH FLOW is the money flowing in and out of the business on a daily basis. A business needs to know this information to make sure it has enough money to cover its expenditure.

## Understanding cash flow

Greg has an art supplies shop.

- Payments from customers are his INFLOWS.

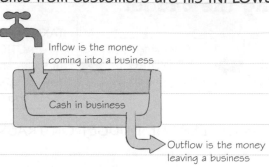

Inflow is the money coming into a business

Cash in business

Outflow is the money leaving a business

- When Greg pays a bill, this is an OUTFLOW.
- The DIFFERENCE is the amount of cash in his business.

If more money is flowing OUT rather than flowing IN, the business may not have enough to pay its staff or suppliers.

## Cash flow forecasting

All businesses need money to pay their bills. They cannot risk running out of cash.

Preparing a CASH FLOW FORECAST allows the business to identify:

- the money that should be coming into a business over a period of time – INFLOW
- the money going out of a business over a period of time – OUTFLOW.

It enables the owner to spot any problems in advance and take action.

If the level of cash (i.e. the DIFFERENCE) is too low at any time, this is a major problem.

## Types of inflows

Bank loans      Sales revenue

**Inflows = money received**

Rents from property the business owns      Share capital invested by the owners

## Types of outflows

Staff wages    Stock or raw materials

Advertising      Fuel for vehicles

**Outflows = payments out**

Telecommunications charges    Insurance and business rates    Rent and utilities

**Worked example**

State **two** advantages to a business of completing a cash flow forecast.   **(2 marks)**

1   The business will know in advance the flow of cash through the business.

2   If cash levels are low at any point, the business can take action promptly.

Remember that cash flow includes inflows and outflows by any payment method, not just in actual notes and coins.

**Now try this**

A business owner is identifying cash outflows for his business.

Which **two** of these are cash outflows?   **(2 marks)**

A ☐ Telephone bill    B ☐ Sales revenue

C ☐ Staff wages    D ☐ Share capital

E ☐ Bank loans

In the online test you may be asked to identify inflows or outflows.

Remember that inflows are **receipts** and outflows are **payments**.

# Calculating net inflows/outflows

Once you know the total inflows and outflows you can calculate NET INFLOWS and NET OUTFLOWS and what the CLOSING CASH BALANCES in the bank will be.

## Net inflows/outflows

This is the DIFFERENCE between total receipts (inflows) and total payments (outflows).

Net inflow/outflow = Inflows − Outflows

Sometimes outflows may be higher than inflows.

| Jane's business | |
|---|---|
| | £ |
| Total receipts | 16,000 |
| Total payments | 10,000 |
| Net inflow | 6,000 |

This shows a NET INFLOW of £6,000.

| Tim's business | |
|---|---|
| | £ |
| Total receipts | 15,000 |
| Total payments | 20,000 |
| Net outflow | (5,000) |

This shows a NET OUTFLOW of £5,000.

It is in brackets because it is a negative amount.

## Net inflow

A NET INFLOW will INCREASE the money already in the bank.

Jane had £2,000 in the bank at the start of March. This is her OPENING BALANCE.

With her net inflow of £6,000, at the end of March she has:

| Jane's business | |
|---|---|
| | £ |
| Opening balance | 2,000 |
| Net inflow | 6,000 |
| Closing balance | 8,000 |

## Net outflow

A NET OUTFLOW will REDUCE the money that is in the bank.

Tim had £3,000 in the bank at the start of March.

With his net outflow of £5,000, at the end of the month he has:

| Tim's business | |
|---|---|
| | £ |
| Opening balance | 3,000 |
| Net outflow | (5,000) |
| Closing Balance | (2,000) |

## Worked example

Jane runs a gym.

Use the information below to complete her cash flow forecast for April. **(2 marks)**

| | April |
|---|---|
| Total receipts | 12,500 |
| Total payments | 10,100 |
| Net inflow | 2,400 |
| Opening balance | 8,000 |
| Closing balance | 10,400 |

Calculate net inflow/outflow **first**.

The closing balance is always the net inflow plus the opening balance.

## Now try this

A business has the following cash flow information for May.

Opening balance: £5,000
Cash inflows: £7,000
Cash outflows: £14,000

What is the **closing balance** for the business at the end of the month? Select **one** answer. **(1 mark)**

A ☐ (£12,000)  B ☐ (£2,000)

C ☐ £9,000  D ☐ £16,000

Remember that brackets around a number mean it is a negative figure.

# Impact of timings on cash flow

The dates when money is received or paid is an important part of managing cash flow as businesses need to manage their budgets around these dates.

## Cash versus credit transactions

- When private customers buy art supplies in Greg's shop they pay immediately. This is a CASH TRANSACTION.
- When schools order art supplies, Greg sends an invoice and asks for payment in 30 days. This is a CREDIT TRANSACTION.

Credit transactions mean Greg has to wait to be paid. If payment is late, or he is not paid at all, this can cause serious problems.

### Late payments

Credit control means chasing up customers who have not paid on time. If a customer is late paying a large debt, the business may have to ask the bank for an overdraft or loan to be able to keep trading.

## Seasonal businesses

Jack has a roundabout. He takes it to fêtes and fairgrounds and rents it for parties.

- In summer, Jack is busy. He has a CASH SURPLUS (cash he can use).
- In winter, Jack earns less but still has bills to pay. He may have a CASH DEFICIT (not enough cash).

He needs to save money he earns in the summer to survive in winter.

Funfairs are an example of a seasonal business.

### Managing/improving inflows

To manage/improve inflows, a business can:
- send out invoices promptly
- chase up late payments
- avoid giving credit to unknown customers
- give discounts for early payment.

### Managing/timing outflows

To manage outflows, a business can:
- delay some payments
- reduce stock levels
- delay a big project
- make cutbacks to reduce expenditure.

## Worked example

Veronica makes designer Christmas crackers. She sells to stores on a credit basis. In August she has a cash flow problem.

> To improve cash flow, identify those actions that will increase inflows and reduce outflows.

| Which **two** of these would help her to improve her cash flow? | **(2 marks)** |

A ☑ Sell online on a cash basis

B ☐ Increase her prices

C ☑ Reduce her expenditure

D ☐ Give longer credit terms

E ☐ Increase stock levels

## Now try this

Jack is owed £5,000 from a customer. Without this money he will have a cash flow problem.

> Recommend **two** actions he can take to manage his finances this month.
> **(2 marks)**

# The benefits of using a cash flow forecast and the risks of not doing it

Cash flow forecasting is a PLANNING TOOL. It helps businesses avoid the risk of serious money problems and to plan for success.

## Benefits of cash flow forecasting

- ✓ The timing of inflows and outflows is known.
- ✓ Possible problems, whether short term or long term, are spotted quickly.
- ✓ Surplus cash can be invested.
- ✓ Expensive items can be bought at the best time.
- ✓ The business can plan to expand or reduce activities.

## Risks of not forecasting cash flow

- ✗ Late inflows may not be identified.
- ✗ There may not be enough cash to pay bills or wages.
- ✗ Suppliers may refuse to trade with the business if they have a reputation for non-payment.
- ✗ A costly emergency loan or overdraft may be needed.
- ✗ The business may run out of money and have to cease trading.

---

### Short-term problems

- Delayed payments from customers.
- Many bills arriving at the same time.
- A large emergency payment.

Action to take:
- Chase up late payments.
- Renegotiate payment dates.
- Obtain a temporary loan.

### Long-term problems

- Too little revenue.
- Expenditure is too high.
- Costs rising steadily.

Action to take:
- Increase sales.
- Widen product range.
- Reduce costs.

---

## Worked example

Megan has started her own business. She has just heard about cash flow forecasting.

> Give **three** benefits of using this as a planning tool.    **(3 marks)**

1  She will be able to check that she always has enough money available to pay her bills.

2  She will be able to spot possible problems and take action to prevent these.

3  If she has any surplus cash at any time she can invest this wisely.

In the online test, check carefully the number of responses you must give.

If it isn't clear from the answer space, check the number of marks allocated. Then make sure you provide enough information to gain all of these.

## Now try this

Jerome has a 'man with a van' business. As people pay him promptly on collection or delivery, he considers a cash flow forecast to be unnecessary.

> Explain **one** way this attitude could put his business at risk.    **(2 marks)**

Start by thinking about the outflows in Jerome's business that he may not always be able to control.

# Completing and analysing cash flow forecasts

Several months' worth of cash flow forecasts are produced at the same time. This is done so that businesses can identify trends and create accurate business plans for the future.

## Completing a cash flow forecast

In March, Megan produced a cash flow forecast for the first time. It included the information shown in the table.

She knows that the CLOSING BALANCE for one month is always the OPENING BALANCE for the next.

|  | March (£) | April (£) |
|---|---|---|
| Total receipts | 8,000 | 6,000 |
| Total payments | 6,500 | 9,500 |
| Net inflow/outflow | 1,500 | (3,500) |
| Opening balance | 1,000 | 2,500 |
| Closing balance | 2,500 | (1,000) |

## Analysing a cash flow forecast

Megan analysed the forecast, starting by looking at the CLOSING BALANCE.

If one month shows a NEGATIVE AMOUNT, Megan should check that column to see if payments are higher than receipts.

Megan has forecast a deficit for April. She should try to reduce her expenditure during that month. If she plans to make a big purchase, she should wait a month or two to see if she has more money.

Action may be needed if the closing balance is too low or too high.

The **bottom line** is very important. Check if the **closing balance** is increasing or decreasing.

## Worked example

Megan has now created a cash flow forecast for the next three months.

Megan wants to buy a new computer in May.

**1** State **one** reason why this would be possible using the information in the table. **(1 mark)**

Megan can afford a computer because her closing balance is £7,500 in May.

|  | May (£) | June (£) | July (£) |
|---|---|---|---|
| Total receipts | 14,000 | 8,000 | 9,000 |
| Total payments | 5,500 | 4,500 | 5,000 |
| Net inflow/outflow | 8,500 | 3,500 | 4,000 |
| Opening balance | (1,000) | 7,500 | 11,000 |
| Closing balance | 7,500 | 11,000 | 15,000 |

**2** Describe **one** way Megan can manage her finances better. **(2 marks)**

Megan's closing balances are steadily increasing. She may benefit from putting some money into a savings account to earn interest.

## Now try this

If you are asked to update a forecast in the online test, you will be given a table with blank cells to complete.

Look at the worked example above. Megan wants to expand her business. Building work will take place in June and July. The builder wants a £7,500 payment in June and the fitters will charge £2,500 in July.

**1** Using this information, update Megan's cash flow forecast. **(4 marks)**

**2** Give **one** reason why you think this is a good time for Megan to plan to expand. **(2 marks)**

# Cost of sales

The COST OF SALES refers to the money it costs to make a product.

## Cost of sales items

- Cost of sales items are things that are used to make a product.
- The exact items will vary, depending on the product made.

You need to know the cost of sales to work out GROSS PROFIT:

$$\frac{\text{GROSS}}{\text{PROFIT}} = \text{REVENUE} - \frac{\text{COST OF}}{\text{SALES}}$$

The cost of sales is DEDUCTED from revenue to find the GROSS PROFIT.

### Jaimie's Jeans

Jaimie designs and makes children's jeans for her company, Jaimie's Jeans. Her raw materials are her cost of sale items, i.e.:
- denim cloth
- fastenings
- zips.

Jaimie makes 1,500 pairs of jeans and the raw materials for each pair costs her £8 to buy.

Her total cost of sales is:

1,500 × £8 = £12,000.

## Worked example

Apprentices in a car factory are learning about the cost of sale items.

Which **one** of these is a cost of sales items for that business?

**(1 mark)**

A ☐ A new roof for the office block

B ☐ Advertising costs for a new model

C ☑ The glass, tyres and steel used in production

D ☐ Transporting new cars to the distribution centre

To identify cost of sale items, think about what is used to **make the product**.

## Now try this

Anya is a florist and makes bouquets. Her trainee, Emily, is puzzled when Anya refers to 'cost of sales'.

**1** Define the term 'cost of sales' for Emily. **(1 mark)**

**2** Identify Anya's **two** cost of sales items from the list below. **(2 marks)**

A ☐ Flowers      B ☐ Ribbon      C ☐ Emily's wage

D ☐ Fuel for the delivery van      E ☐ Rent

**3** Explain **one** reason why Anya needs to know how much she spends on cost of sale items. **(2 marks)**

# Gross profit

GROSS PROFIT is how much money is left from selling an item, after you have deducted the cost of making it.

## Defining gross profit

GROSS PROFIT is the money made from selling a product (REVENUE) after the cost of producing it (COST OF SALES) has been deducted.

You practised calculating revenue on page 6.

## Calculating gross profit

You can use this formula to calculate gross profit:

GROSS PROFIT = REVENUE – COST OF SALES

You need to learn the formula for gross profit. It will not be given to you in the online test.

---

### Jaimie's gross profit

Jaimie makes children's fashion jeans. Last year she sold 1,500 pairs at £25 each.

1   Her REVENUE is:

    1,500 × £25 = £37,500.

2   Jaimie's COST OF SALES was calculated on page 21. Each pair cost her £8 to make so her total cost of sales was £12,000.

3   Jaimie's GROSS PROFIT is therefore:

    £37,500 – £12,000 = £25,500.

---

### Worked example

Last year, a business earned £80,000 in revenue. Its cost of sales was £20,000.

> Calculate the gross profit for this business. **(1 mark)**

```
Gross profit = £80,000 - £20,000 = £60,000
```

You can always check how much time you have left in the online test by clicking on the 'time' button.

---

### Now try this

A garden centre sells plants and sheds.

- Its revenue from plants last year was £60,000 and its cost of sales was £15,000.
- Its revenue from sheds was £80,000 and its cost of sales was £25,000.

> Calculate the **gross profit** for this business.    **(2 marks)**

Calculate one item at a time.

1   Work out the gross profit for plants.

2   Work out the gross profit for sheds.

3   Add them together.

In the test make sure you use the working box to show your calculation.

# The impact of positive and negative gross profit

A business needs a POSITIVE GROSS PROFIT to survive. A NEGATIVE GROSS PROFIT results in a loss.

## Positive gross profit

This is when revenue is MORE than the cost of sales, for example:

| Revenue | – Cost of sales | = Positive gross profit |
|---|---|---|
| £60,000 | £40,000 | £20,000 |

## Negative gross profit

This is when the revenue is LESS than the cost of sales, for example:

| Revenue | – Cost of sales | = Negative gross profit |
|---|---|---|
| £25,000 | £30,000 | (£5,000) |

A negative gross profit means the business has made a **loss**.

## The impact of positive gross profit

Positive gross profit is GOOD NEWS. The business has the potential to do well.

It means that:

- ✓ there is money to pay for expenses
- ✓ there may be money available for better equipment or expansion
- ✓ the cost of sales is not too high
- ✓ enough goods are being sold to produce a profit.

## The impact of negative gross profit

Negative gross profit is BAD NEWS. The business cannot survive if this continues.

It means that:

- ✗ there is no money to pay expenses or wages without a loan or overdraft – which increases costs
- ✗ the cost of sales is too high – this could be reduced by buying cheaper supplies
- ✗ sales revenue is too low – more goods must be sold.

## Worked example

Laura has made a negative gross profit.

**1** Outline what this means. **(1 mark)**

A negative gross profit means that her cost of sales is higher than her revenue. She has no money left to pay her expenses.

Give a simple definition to outline 'negative gross profit'. Then state the actions needed to improve the situation.

**2** Identify **two** actions she could take to improve this situation. **(2 marks)**

**1** Increase her sales volumes by selling more goods.

**2** Reduce her cost of sales, for example by changing her suppliers.

## Now try this

Tariq has just started his own business and is learning about gross profit.

**1** Explain **one** reason why positive gross profit is important to a business. **(2 marks)**

**2** State **two** issues he must address if he makes a negative gross profit. **(2 marks)**

# Net profit

NET PROFIT is the amount you have left after you have deducted your expenses from your GROSS PROFIT.

## Defining net profit

Net profit is the money made from selling a product after all costs (expenditure) have been deducted.

## Calculating net profit

You can use this formula to calculate net profit.

NET PROFIT = GROSS PROFIT − EXPENDITURE

You need to learn the formula for net profit. It will NOT be given in the online test.

## Net profit for Jaimie's Jeans

1. Jaimie has added up her EXPENDITURE for her Jaimie's Jeans business from last year. This included her overheads (such as rent, electricity, telephone) and advertising costs. The total was £12,000.
2. Jaimie's GROSS PROFIT was £25,000.
3. Her NET PROFIT is: £25,000 − £12,000 = £13,000.

## Worked example

Darren has started his own business. He has identified the following information from his business:

| Income from sales | £19,000 |
|---|---|
| Cost of sales | £4,000 |
| Expenses | £3,500 |

Using this information, calculate:

**(a)** Darren's gross profit　　**(1 mark)**

£19,000 − £4,000 = £15,000

**(b)** Darren's net profit　　**(1 mark)**

£15,000 − £3,500 = £11,500

In the online test, if you want to come back to a question later, use the 'flag' button. It will then appear as a flagged question in your review screen at the end of the test so you won't forget it.

## Now try this

Sahida makes homemade chutneys and sauces. She wants to sell these at craft fairs. She says she is confused by the terms 'gross profit' and 'net profit' and has asked for your help.

Define each of these terms for Sahida.　　**(2 marks)**

# The impact of positive and negative net profit

NET PROFIT is the amount of money left to reward the owner or to REINVEST in the business.

## Positive net profit

This is when gross profit is MORE than expenditure.

| Gross profit | − Expenditure | = Positive net profit |
|---|---|---|
| £25,000 | £10,000 | £15,000 |

## Negative net profit

This is when gross profit is LESS than expenditure.

| Gross profit | − Expenditure | = Negative net profit |
|---|---|---|
| £25,000 | £30,000 | (£5,000) |

### The impact of positive net profit

Positive net profit is GOOD NEWS.

It means that:
- ✓ gross profit is positive
- ✓ expenditure is less than gross profit
- ✓ the business has money it can use to expand or improve.

### The impact of negative net profit

Negative net profit is BAD NEWS.

It means that:
- ✗ gross profit is low or negative
- ✗ expenditure is too high
- ✗ the business is losing money.

## Worked example

Ivan has calculated that he has made a negative net profit.

Identify **two** actions he could take to improve this situation. **(2 marks)**

A ✓ Buy raw materials from cheaper suppliers
B ☐ Buy new equipment
C ✓ Reduce his overheads
D ☐ Employ more staff
E ☐ Spend more on advertising

- Buying cheaper raw materials will improve both gross profit and net profit.
- To improve Ivan's net profit, you also need to identify how he can **spend less** on running his business.

## Now try this

Oliver is a photographer. His gross profit was £25,000 last year but his net profit was only £7,000. He is baffled as he thought his business was doing well.

1 Explain why Oliver's net profit is lower than his gross profit. **(1 mark)**

2 Identify **one** way Oliver can improve his net profit. **(1 mark)**

# Financial statements

FINANCIAL STATEMENTS show whether or not a business is doing well.

## The purpose of financial statements

- They record the financial activities of a business.
- They provide an immediate overview of the business' financial position.
- They show whether or not the business is well managed and successful.

Some types of business must produce financial statements by law.

Competitiors   Shareholders   Managers

**Who reads financial statements?**

The government

Customers   Suppliers

Employees

For example, shareholders want to know their money is safe and the business is well managed.

## Types of financial statements

The TWO you must know are:

**1** the INCOME STATEMENT (PROFIT AND LOSS ACCOUNT) – this shows profit or loss

**2** the STATEMENT OF FINANCIAL POSITION (BALANCE SHEET) – this lists assets and liabilities.

## Key terms

- ASSETS are items owned by the business that are worth money.
- LIABILITIES are debts or obligations that the business has.

## Worked example

Identify **two** types of information shown in financial documents. **(2 marks)**

A ☐ Employees' salaries   B ☑ Gross and net profit

C ☐ Forecast sales figures   D ☑ Assets and liabilities

E ☐ The break-even point

You can navigate backwards and forwards in the online test and change any answers you want in the time allowed.

## Now try this

Paula wants an overdraft. The bank has asked her to bring some financial documents with her.

1 Identify **two** financial documents she should take. **(2 marks)**

2 Give **two** reasons why the bank wants to see these documents. **(2 marks)**

# Income statement (profit and loss account)

An INCOME STATEMENT (PROFIT AND LOSS ACCOUNT) shows the PROFIT or LOSS made by the business over a period of time (usually one year).

## The format of an income statement (profit and loss account)

|  | £ | £ |
|---|---|---|
| Income from sales |  | 40,000 |
| Cost of sales | 10,000 |  |
| Gross profit |  | 30,000 |
| **Expenses** |  |  |
| Wages | 13,000 |  |
| Electricity | 2,000 |  |
| Net profit |  | 15,000 |

The top part is the TRADING ACCOUNT. It shows that gross profit = income from sales − cost of sales.

The next part lists expenses and overheads.

The NET PROFIT is calculated by subtracting the TOTAL EXPENSES from the gross profit.

The middle column shows the COST OF SALES and EXPENSES.

The right-hand column shows INCOME FROM SALES and PROFIT.

The information gives gross profit first, then net profit.

If you have to complete an income statement (profit and loss account) in the online test you will be given all the information you need. You must then enter it in the right place in the statement.

## Worked example

**1** Enter the following items into the income statement (profit and loss account) for a business. **(2 marks)**

- Income from sales = £220,000
- Cost of sales = £130,000
- Wages and salaries = £32,000
- Utilities = £15,000

Use the figures to calculate the gross and net profit, if these are not shown.

You have a calculator function you can use in the online test.

**2** Using this information, complete the other parts of the income statement. To help you, some information has already been entered. **(2 marks)**

|  | £ | £ |
|---|---|---|
| Income from sales |  | 220,000 |
| Cost of sales | 130,000 |  |
| Gross profit |  | 90,000 |
| **Expenses** |  |  |
| Wages and salaries | 32,000 |  |
| Utilities | 15,000 |  |
| Net profit |  | 43,000 |

## Now try this

Cathy makes cupcakes. She has just finished trading for her first year.

Using her figures below, prepare an income statement (profit and loss account), using the correct format and identifying her gross and net profit. **(3 marks)**

Income from sales = £28,000    Cost of sales = £8,000

Utilities = £4,000    Car expenses = £2,400

# Assets, liabilities and working capital

The ASSETS and LIABILITIES of a business need to be included in the statement of financial position (balance sheet). They also enable you to calculate the WORKING CAPITAL.

## Assets

ASSETS are items the business OWNS or money OWED TO the business and include:

- FIXED ASSETS: these are needed for the business to be able to trade, for example, a van or computer
- CURRENT ASSETS: assets which are cash or which can easily be converted to cash. They are broken down into:
  - STOCK which is sold to customers
  - CASH received from customers and paid out to buy new stock
- TRADE RECEIVABLES (debtors): the term for customers who owe money.

## Liabilities

LIABILITIES are DEBTS OWED BY the business and include:

- CURRENT LIABILITIES: debts that must be paid soon. They are broken down into:
  - TRADE PAYABLES (creditors): for example, suppliers that the business must pay
  - OVERDRAFTS or short-term BANK LOANS
- LONG-TERM LIABILITIES: funds borrowed over a long time, such as ten years.

## Working capital (net current assets)

WORKING CAPITAL is the money the business needs every day to trade.

The current assets should always be MORE than the current liabilities.

This means that if all the short-term debts were paid there would still be money left.

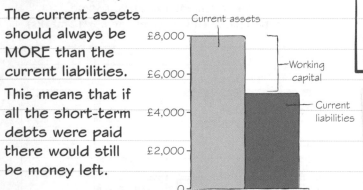

### Calculating working capital

You can use this formula to calculate working capital:

$$\text{Working capital} = \text{Current assets} - \text{Current liabilities}$$

Another name for this is NET CURRENT ASSETS.

Sean has £6,500 in the bank and customers owe him £1,500, so his current assets are £8,000. He owes suppliers £5,000. His working capital is:

£8,000 − £5,000 = £3,000

## Worked example

Keiron is a handyman. He wants to complete his statement of financial position. He needs to identify which items are liabilities.

Which **two** of these are liabilities?    **(2 marks)**

- A ☐ Customers who owe money
- B ☐ His van
- C ☑ Overdraft
- D ☑ Money owed to suppliers

## Now try this

Keiron is confused by some terms.

Identify **one** of the differences between:
- A fixed assets and current assets
- B trade receivables and trade payables.    **(2 marks)**

Answer this question by identifying the main difference between each term.

# The statement of financial position (balance sheet)

This is a financial snapshot of the assets and liabilities of the business on a particular day.

## The purpose of a statement of financial position (balance sheet)

The financial position of the business at a specific point in time

**The statement of financial position (balance sheet) shows:**

How the business has spent its money, i.e. the assets it has bought

How the business is funded, i.e. where it gets its capital from

### Key terms

The heading SHAREHOLDERS' FUNDS on the statement of financial position is for:

- CAPITAL – money from internal sources such as shareholders or from external sources such as bank loans
- RETAINED PROFIT – earlier profits the owner has kept in the business; an internal source of capital.

## The format of the statement of financial position (balance sheet)

Martina runs an online business. This is her statement of financial position (balance sheet).

| ASSETS | £ | £ |
|---|---|---|
| **Fixed assets** | | |
| Computer | | 1,000 |
| **Current assets** | | |
| Stock | 4,000 | |
| Trade receivables | 600 | |
| Cash in bank | 2,000 | 6,600 |
| **Total assets** | | 7,600 |
| LIABILITIES | | |
| **Current liabilities** | | |
| Trade payables | 700 | |
| Overdraft | 300 | 1,000 |
| **Working capital** (Net current assets) | | 5,600 |
| **Total assets less current liabilities** | | 6,600 |
| **Shareholders' funds** | | |
| Share capital | 5,000 | |
| Retained profit | 1,600 | |
| | | 6,600 |

There is no need to include the £ signs before the numbers in these columns, because they are given as the column headings.

Calculate working capital by subtracting the **current liabilities** from the **current assets**.

The **total assets** less **current liabilities** are the same as the **shareholders funds**.

## Worked example

Refer to the statement above for Martina's online business.

Identify **two** assets that Martina bought with the capital she invested in the business. **(2 marks)**

```
Martina bought a computer for
£1,000. She has also bought
stock valued at £4,000.
```

## Now try this

First, identify his current assets and liabilities and then do the calculation.

Mo is a decorator. Mo's van is worth £4,000. He has an overdraft of £200 and he owes his suppliers £800. He has £5,000 in the bank and customers owe him £300.

1 Identify **one** current liability. **(1 mark)**

2 Calculate his working capital. **(3 marks)**

# Completing a statement of financial position (balance sheet)

You may need to complete or calculate blank spaces in a statement of financial position (balance sheet).

### Online test

In the online test, you may have to complete a statement of financial position (balance sheet) or make calculations of:
• current and total assets
• working capital
• total assets less current liabilities.

You may be give information on:
• assets – fixed or current
• liabilities – current or long term
• amounts owed BY trade receivables (ASSETS)
• amounts owed TO trade payables (LIABILITIES).

## Worked example

Priti produces customised stationery and is completing her statement of financial position (balance sheet) for her first year. She has entered the £5,000 she invested in the business under shareholders' funds. Her assets are:
• a van worth £1,500     • stock worth £3,000     • £1,000 in the bank.

Using this information, complete the statement of financial position (balance sheet).     **(2 marks)**

To help you, some information has already been entered.

| ASSETS | £ | £ |
|---|---|---|
| **Fixed assets** | | |
| Van | | 1,500 |
| **Current assets** | | |
| Stock | 3,000 | |
| Trade receivables | 200 | |
| Cash in bank | 1,000 | 4,200 |
| **Total assets** | | 5,700 |
| LIABILITIES | | |
| **Current liabilities** | | |
| Trade payables | 600 | |
| Overdraft | 100 | 700 |
| **Working capital** (Net current assets) | | 3,500 |
| **Total assets less current liabilities** | | 5,000 |
| **Shareholders' funds** | | |
| Share capital | 5,000 | |

The working capital is calculated by subtracting the current liabilities from the current assets.

The total assets less current liabilities figure is the same as the shareholders' funds if calculations are correct.

## Now try this

Look at the worked example above. Priti buys equipment for £750 by paying £500 in cash and increasing her overdraft by £250.

Note that Priti's working capital will go down by the amount she has spent – £750.

Prepare a new statement of financial position that includes this information.     **(4 marks)**

# Increasing profits and analysing an income statement (profit and loss account)

Businesses must increase profits if their income statement (profit and loss account) shows these are low.

## Increasing profit

To increase profits, a business can focus on two areas: increasing revenue or lowering costs.

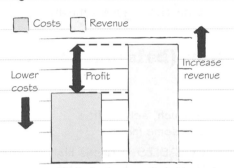

The business may focus on:
- increasing its gross profit and/or
- increasing its net profit.

### Potential pitfalls

- Buying cheaper raw materials may reduce the quality of the goods.
- Paying lower wages could lose staff.
- Increasing the selling price could mean fewer sales.
- More advertising can increase costs.

## Increasing gross profit

 **1** Reduce cost of sales by:
- negotiating cheaper prices with suppliers
- using different (cheaper) materials.

**2** Increase sales revenue by:
- selling more items
- increasing the selling price (if possible).

## Increasing net profit

**1** Reduce expenses by:
- identifying those expenses that are too high
- taking appropriate action, for example:
  - utilities/telecoms: change supplier
  - rent/rates: move to cheaper premises
  - wages: reduce number of staff/ pay lower rates/employ part-time workers.

## Worked example

The figures in the table below are from Asiya's income statement (profit and loss account) in 2013.

| Sales revenue | £250,000 |
|---|---|
| Rent | £30,000 |
| Cost of sales | £200,000 |
| Staff wages | £60,000 |
| Gas bill | £20,000 |

You can quickly check Asiya's gross profit by deducting cost of sales from sales revenue.

 Remember that brackets around a profit mean a negative amount. Asiya's business has made a **loss**.

Her net profit for this business is (£60,000) for the year.

Identify **two** areas she should improve to increase her net profit in 2014. **(2 marks)**

**1** Her cost of sales is high in relation to her sales revenue — her gross profit is only £50,000.

**2** Her gas bill also seems high for a small business.

## Now try this

Look at the worked example.

For **each** of the areas identified as needing improvement, suggest what Asiya should do. **(2 marks)**

# Analysing a statement of financial position (balance sheet) for a small business

Analysis of a statement of financial position (balance sheet) involves assessing each figure in the statement to see where improvements can be made.

## Analysing an extract

You may be shown an extract from an income statement (profit and loss account), as on page 30, or a statement of financial position (balance sheet), as here.

If you are asked to ANALYSE this, you should look at the figures shown in the example below and think about what these mean for the business. Make sure you know what all the figures mean.

## Marianne's statement of financial position (balance sheet)

|  | £ | £ |
|---|---|---|
| **Fixed assets** |  |  |
| Motor vehicle |  | 5,000 |
| **Current assets** |  |  |
| Stock | 6,000 |  |
| Trade receivables | 7,000 |  |
| Cash in bank | 250 | 13,250 |
|  |  |  |
| **Current liabilities** |  |  |
| Trade payables | 4,500 |  |
| Overdraft | 8,000 |  |
| **Working capital** |  |  |
| (Net current assets) |  | 750 |

STOCK: too much, sell it off; too little, buy some more.

TRADE RECEIVABLES: if this is high then collect payments from debtors.

CASH: if this is low, chase up debts or sell off slow-moving stock.

TRADE PAYABLES: if debts to suppliers are high, they may stop providing goods.

OVERDRAFT: banks charge for this, so pay it off as soon as possible.

WORKING CAPITAL: this needs to be enough to run the business.

## Worked example

Marianne has spent one year in business and has shown you an extract from her statement of financial position (balance sheet). This is shown above.

> Analyse this and describe **two** short-term actions she should take to improve her business's position for next year.   **(4 marks)**

1 | Marianne's stock is too high and her cash is too low. If she held a discount sale to sell off slow-moving items she could increase her cash.

There may be a number of areas that are weak. Identify enough, two in this case, to answer the question and say what should be done.

2 | Marianne is owed £7,000 by her customers. She should get these people to pay her as soon as possible to reduce this amount.

## Now try this

Look at the worked example above.

> Describe **two** other ways that Marianne can strengthen her business further.
> **(4 marks)**

# Exam skills 1

You will have one hour to answer the onscreen test. There are 50 marks. There will be questions on ALL the learning aims: A, B and C. You can answer the questions in any order.

## Question types

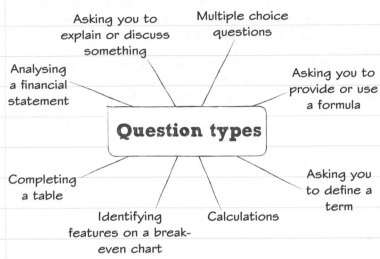

Asking you to explain or discuss something

Multiple choice questions

Analysing a financial statement

Asking you to provide or use a formula

**Question types**

Completing a table

Asking you to define a term

Identifying features on a break-even chart

Calculations

## Understanding the question

Read each question carefully. Make sure you know exactly what you have to do.

### Always check

- how many items you must select or identify
- you understand the term(s) being used (for example, fixed or variable costs; net profit or gross profit)
- how you must respond (for example, click on an answer, complete white cells in a table or type in a box).

## Hints and tips

**1** Revise key terms and formulae you need to know.

**2** Arrive in good time for the test.

**3** If you feel panicky, read through a few questions at the start.

**4** You do not need a pen or paper for the online test.

## Worked example

Raynor makes wooden puzzles and sells these to retail businesses for £6 each. Last year he sold 18,000 puzzles.

**1** Calculate his **total revenue**.    **(1 mark)**

> 18,000 × £6 = £108,000

This question tests that you know the formula for revenue is: number of sales × price per unit.

**2** Which **two** of these are variable costs in his business?    **(2 marks)**

A ☐ Monthly rent    B ☑ Wood    C ☑ Small boxes

D ☐ Telephone bill    E ☐ Property insurance

Remember that variable costs are directly related to how items are made and packed.

**3** Explain how Raynor will calculate his **profit**.    **(2 marks)**

> Raynor needs to know his revenue and his expenditure. He can then use the formula:
> Profit = revenue − expenditure.

This question tests whether you know the formula for profit.

# Exam skills 2

It is important to familiarise yourself with the features of the online test.

TIME: this shows/hides the time that has elapsed since the start of the test. Find it at the bottom right of your screen.

HELP: this tells you about the features of the test and the tools available. It does not provide technical help. If you have a technical problem in the online test then tell the invigilator straight away.

ACCESSIBILITY PANEL: if you are struggling to read the screen, try adjusting the colours or magnifying the screen.

NEXT: this moves the test on to the next question.

WORKING BOX: use the working box for rough notes or calculations at any time. This text will not be marked.

CALCULATOR: use this when you have to carry out any calculations.

REVIEW: this button lets you go back through the test and check your answers. Any questions you 'flagged' show on this screen.

FLAG: you can do the questions in any order. If one puzzles you, leave it and carry on. Use the 'flag' button to mark it, so you won't forget about it.

PREVIOUS: this moves the test back to the previous question.

QUIT: when you click this button a pop-up window asks if you want to quit the test. Answer 'yes' or 'no'. If you press 'no' you return to the question you were answering.

## Worked example

Jasmine plans to start a small shop selling frozen yoghurt.

**1** Give **two** examples of start-up costs the business may have. **(2 marks)**

> A freezer and a cash register.

Study the **context** so you make appropriate suggestions.

Jasmine's predicted figures for next year are:

| Selling price per frozen yoghurt | £1.50 |
|---|---|
| Variable cost per item | 25p |
| Fixed costs | £6,000 |

The formula to calculate breakeven is:

$$\text{Breakeven} = \frac{\text{Fixed costs}}{\text{Selling price per unit} - \text{Variable costs per unit}}$$

**2** How many frozen yoghurts does Jasmine need to sell to **break even**? **(1 mark)**

> 4,800

Remember, in the online test, you will have a box to show your working.

**3** Outline the difference between the break-even point and a margin of safety. **(2 marks)**

> The break-even point is the number of products that must be sold for the business to cover its costs. The margin of safety is the difference between the break-even point and a higher target sales figure that is set so that the business will make a profit.

Show the difference by describing one term and then the other. These are important terms to know.

# Exam skills 3

## Revision topics

Before the test make sure you know:

- ✓ the difference between key terms, for example: start-up/running costs; fixed/variable costs; assets/liabilities; and net/gross profit
- ✓ the features of a break-even chart and how to use the breakeven formula
- ✓ formulae for revenue, total costs and profit
- ✓ the items on a cash flow forecast, income statement (profit and loss account) and statement of financial position (balance sheet)
- ✓ what is meant by cost of sales and working capital
- ✓ how to improve gross and net profit
- ✓ the benefits of these planning tools: breakeven analysis, cash flow forecasts and budgeting/budget control, and the risks of not doing these.

### Hints and tips

- Use the marks given for a question to guide you on your answer. If you are asked for four points and you only give two, you cannot get full marks.
- You may be asked to type your answer in a box. The size of the box is important. If it is a large box and there are several marks, this means a more detailed answer is required. The box will scroll down as you type.

## What does 'discuss' mean?

Discuss means identifying the benefits of doing something and the risks involved in not doing it or taking action. You have to demonstrate that you understand all the different aspects of the question.

## Collecting marks

Always remember that you will never lose marks for something that is incorrect. You can only **gain** marks in the test. For that reason, if you think something may be correct then it is worth including it.

## Worked example

The trading account is the top part of the income statement. It is just the gross profit formula as a table. Sales revenue − cost of sales = gross profit.

Sophie is preparing a trading account.

**1** Use the information below to complete this.
Cost of sales £22,000    Income from sales £72,000    **(2 marks)**

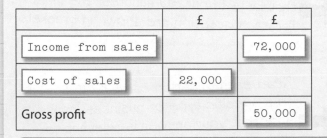

|  | £ | £ |
|---|---|---|
| Income from sales |  | 72,000 |
| Cost of sales | 22,000 |  |
| Gross profit |  | 50,000 |

The answer shows that the learner clearly understands the link between gross and net profit and how businesses can improve both.

**2** Discuss how preparing a trading account can benefit a business.    **(6 marks)**

A trading account shows gross profit. A business can check that they are not spending too much money on cost of sales and that it is earning enough sales revenue.

Gross profit is important because this is needed to pay for expenses, including staff wages. If gross profit is too low to cover these then the business may be losing money and may not survive.

If the gross profit is too low it must try to increase sales income or lower the cost of sales. It could hold special events to attract more customers or try to find cheaper suppliers or negotiate savings and discounts on some items. It could increase prices but this could result in customers going elsewhere. It is better off trying not to spend more money if possible.

# Defining marketing and its importance to business

## The importance of marketing to businesses

Marketing involves identifying and understanding the needs and wants of current and future customers. Businesses can then provide products and services that meet these needs and make a PROFIT for the business.

Build their image and reputation

Develop/sell the right products to meet customer needs

Gain/increase market share

**Marketing helps businesses to:**

Develop customer loyalty

Launch a new product/business and boost sales

Develop brand recognition

## The meaning of marketing

Marketing involves understanding the customers' needs and ensuring that they are the most important thing to the business. This should be reflected in everything the business and its staff do and say.

Marketing is NOT just selling or advertising. Selling is exchanging goods or services for money. Advertising is just one way of making customers aware of a product or service.

### Key terms

- CUSTOMERS are people who purchase for themselves or for others.
- MARKET SHARE is the percentage of the total sales of a product accounted for by one company.

## Worked example

Alyson wants to open a boutique selling vintage clothes.

Identify **two** ways in that she will benefit from using marketing. **(2 marks)**

1 Marketing will enable Alyson to establish her business so that her shop and brand is known by customers.

2 It will help her to understand her customers' needs and stock the right clothes and accessories to meet these needs.

The Unit 9 test is a paper-based exam that lasts 1 hour 30 minutes. The marks for each question are shown in brackets.

Read each question carefully. If it relates to a specific type of business, make sure that your answer is relevant to that context. Here Alyson will be selling clothes in a shop, not making a product in a factory or workshop.

## Now try this

Define the term 'marketing'. **(1 mark)**

Your definition should include 'identifying and meeting customers' needs' and 'doing this profitably'.

# How businesses use marketing

Businesses use marketing to launch new products, boost flagging sales, keep customer loyalty, promote their brand or penetrate new markets. There are four other main ways they use marketing:

**1 To understand customer needs**

- Who are our target customers?
- What are their needs?
- How can we meet these?

**2 To keep ahead of competitors**

- Who are our competitors?
- What do they offer?
- How can we make our product better or more appealing so that we gain COMPETITIVE ADVANTAGE?

**3 To communicate effectively with the public**

- What are the best CHANNELS to use (for example, TV, press, email)?
- What message(s) will attract and keep people's attention?

**4 To increase sales and profitability**

- How can we offer value for money?
- What benefits can we give our customers?

£ Reducing prices will simply lower profits, not increase them, if sales levels remain the same.

---

## Worked example

Stefan has an idea for a new product.

Give **two** reasons why he should use marketing before he spends money developing his idea.
**(2 marks)**

1 He needs to understand the needs of his customers and check if his idea would meet these needs.

2 He needs to check if a similar product is already made and on the market and plan to make his own product different or more appealing.

The Unit 9 test has two sections: A and B. In section B all the questions relate to one detailed case study.

Other acceptable answers would have been, he needs:
- to identify his target customers
- to find out how to communicate with his potential customers and give the right information
- to help him decide what price he could charge.

---

## Now try this

A UK business decides to sell its products overseas.

Describe **two** ways that it could use marketing to penetrate new markets successfully.
**(4 marks)**

# Marketing, corporate objectives and SMART objectives

CORPORATE OBJECTIVES state the aims the business wants to achieve, such as increasing market share, selling overseas, increasing profits and/or improving customer relations. MARKETING contributes to achieving these objectives.

## The marketing plan

This identifies the marketing activities which must be completed to achieve the aims of the business.

The marketing plan must reflect the corporate objectives.

## SMART objectives

Objectives need to be SMART:

- **S**pecific – they give an exact numerical target to achieve
- **M**easurable – they are easily measured
- **A**chievable – they can be achieved with the available resources
- **R**ealistic – they are possible for that business to achieve
- **T**ime-based – they have a deadline for achievement.

### Example of a SMART objective

Corporate objective: increase profits by 5%

↓

SMART marketing objective: increase online sales by 5% in 12 months

## Worked example

Explain **one** way corporate objectives impact the marketing plan. **(2 marks)**

Corporate objectives state the aims of the business, such as to increase sales by 5 per cent or to open six new branches next year. These will affect the content of the marketing plan which lists marketing activities that must be carried out to achieve these aims.

Think of this in stages.

1 Start with the aims of the business (its corporate objectives).

2 Decide what marketing activities are needed to achieve these aims.

3 Write these down in the marketing plan.

4 Check that all objectives are SMART.

## Now try this

Jen runs a successful sandwich shop in a busy town centre. Her competition has recently been increasing but she thinks if she offers a wider range of food, including sushi, then she could do well.

She writes the following objective: to increase sales by 5 per cent.

Identify **one** way Jen could improve this objective to make sure it is SMART.
**(1 mark)**

Start by checking which SMART criteria this objective meets and which it doesn't!

# B2B and B2C markets

There are many different types of market. A business must decide which type of market it is targeting, as this will affect the marketing activities it carries out.

## Business to business (B2B) market

BUSINESS TO BUSINESS is selling to industrial buyers or retailers. Goods may be raw materials, equipment, consumables or items for resale.

Trade fairs are an important way of selling in the B2B market.

## Business to consumer (B2C) market

BUSINESS TO CONSUMER is selling to private individuals and households – in a shop, online, door to door, or in their own home.

A bakery is an example of a B2C business.

## B2B marketing activities

- Presentations to industry buyers
- Visits by sales representatives to firms
- Stands at trade fairs
- Networking with contacts.

Business buyers are concerned with high volumes/bulk orders, price, finance and credit terms, benefits, delivery service/dates and after-sales support.

## B2C marketing activities

- Market research about customers
- Establishing a memorable brand
- Advertising the brand
- Promotions to tempt people to buy.

Consumers require smaller quantities and good customer service. This means that the business needs to focus on its reputation, gaining competitive advantage and increasing market share.

## Worked example

A business makes catering equipment.
Outline **two** ways it should market its goods to hotels and hospitals. **(2 marks)**

1 It should employ sales representatives who will make appointments to see buyers. They will provide the buyers with information and arrange presentations and demonstrations.

2 It should have a stand at a trade fair so that industrial buyers can see its new products and their features.

Businesses that supply the B2B market make it as easy as possible for customers to buy from them by:
- visiting them
- arranging finance and delivery
- offering credit terms
- providing after-sales support.

Some businesses, such as banks, solicitors, surveyors and decorators, deal with both markets,.

## Now try this

A local greengrocer decides to increase business by offering to supply fruit and vegetables to local care homes.

Give **two** examples of how his marketing activities may now change. **(2 marks)**

Think about how he can impress B2B buyers.

# Other types of markets

Markets can be divided into segments in several other ways. This makes it easier for businesses to target the market they want to supply. Three other types of market are:

## 1 Goods and services markets

- The GOODS MARKET is concerned with PRODUCTS – from apples to xylophones.
- The SERVICES market is concerned with services – from car valeting to window cleaning.

Some businesses operate in BOTH these markets.

## 2 Capital and consumer goods markets

- CAPITAL GOODS are machines and tools used by industry during production, such as forklift trucks or bottling equipment.
- CONSUMER GOODS are items bought in shops or online by customers for themselves or someone else.

## 3 Niche and mass markets

- A NICHE MARKET is a small market that aims to meet specific user needs – for example, a group of customers for a specialist product, such as gluten-free bread.
- The MASS MARKET is the largest market possible for a product.

The market for biscuits is a mass market.

## Consumers or customers?

- CONSUMERS are people who consume or use an item. They are the END USER.
- CUSTOMERS – whether private individuals or businesses – make the purchase. They may use the item, sell it or give it away.

At Christmas, many customers buy gifts for other consumers or end users.

## Worked example

Give **two** reasons why small businesses often target a niche market.  **(2 marks)**

1 A small business will not have the resources to supply goods on a large scale so it is better to focus on a small market.

2 Large businesses prefer the mass market as they want to sell large quantities, so there will be less competition for a small business if it focuses on supplying a niche market.

Large scale producers usually make goods for the mass market. This provides opportunities for small producers to focus on niche markets, where there is more scope for being different and less competition from large firms.

## Now try this

Define the term 'capital goods'.  **(1 mark)**

# Business models

A BUSINESS MODEL is the way in which a business makes money or adds value. You need to know about the following three types of business model.

## 1 The sales model

| Focus: | SELLING GOODS. |
|---|---|
| Revenue: | Comes from SALES. |
| ✓ Benefits: | Staff often get bonuses and commission. Customers get low prices. |
| ✗ Drawbacks: | Customers can only choose from goods on offer. |
| Example: | Cosmetics sold at parties. |

Customers can get low-priced cosmetics through the sales model.

## 2 The advertising model

| Focus: | Obtaining revenue from ADVERTS or SPONSORS. |
|---|---|
| Revenue: | Comes from ADVERTISERS. |
| ✓ Benefits: | Advertisers reach their target market easily; the business gets paid. |
| ✗ Drawbacks: | The business has no control over advertisers withdrawing adverts. |
| Examples: | Commercial radio, commercial TV (e.g. ITV) and satellite TV (e.g. Sky). |

## 3 The marketing model

| Focus: | MEETING CUSTOMER NEEDS/ BUILDING CUSTOMER RELATIONSHIPS. |
|---|---|
| Revenue: | Comes from sales to LOYAL CUSTOMERS. |
| ✓ Benefits: | The customer gets excellent service; the business gets higher sales. |
| ✗ Drawbacks: | Meeting individual customer needs can be time-consuming and costs money. |
| Example: | Small, independent businesses often use the marketing model. |

## A mixture of models

Many businesses operate more than one model.

For example, Sky TV gets revenue from advertisers and from customer subscriptions. It also screens programmes customers want to watch and offers benefits, such as allowing downloading of programmes to other devices.

Free, fast delivery is demanded by many customers to meet their needs.

### Worked example

Safiyah sells children's books at parties and school fairs. She is sent books by the publisher and gets commission on sales she makes.

**1** What business model does the publisher operate? **(1 mark)**

The publisher operates the sales model.

**2** Identify **one** advantage and **one** disadvantage of this business model. **(2 marks)**

An advantage is that prices are usually cheap, which encourages sales.
A disadvantage is that a customer may not like the books on offer so may not buy.

Read the scenario carefully. Identify the business model by identifying the main way in which the business makes its money. This publisher makes money from selling children's books.

### Now try this

Identify the business model used for each of the following: **A** a TV shopping channel; **B** a single father with promotions for single-parent holidays on his blog; **C** a landscape gardener.

**(3 marks)**

# Business orientation and choice of business model

Businesses may be MARKET ORIENTATED or PRODUCT ORIENTATED. This will affect their choice of business model.

## Market-orientated businesses

These businesses identify the needs of their prospective customer, then make or sell the product (or provide the service) to meet these needs.

They are more likely to operate a marketing business model.

### Example: John Lewis

John Lewis is a market-orientated business. In 2013, it started selling pet supplies in response to customer demand. It also operates a marketing model with its promise 'Never knowingly undersold'.

John Lewis started selling pet supplies in response to demand.

## Product-orientated businesses

These businesses focus on their areas of expertise to produce innovative items.

They are more likely to operate a sales or advertising model.

### Example: Google

Google is a product-orientated business. It has developed Google Glass and a driverless car. It operates an advertising business model through paid searches on its search engine.

Google Glass is an innovative product.

## Worked example

Pam sells her fashion jewellery online and asked friends and customers for advice when sales were poor. They said many items were too elaborate. They also suggested she sold at craft fairs where people could see and handle her jewellery.

Describe **one** impact Pam's business orientation has on her business. **(2 marks)**

Pam's business has a marketing orientation because she is interested in the views of her customers and finding out what they think. This then influences what she produces and where she sells her products.

You should try to make two points when answering a 'describe' question like this one.

## Changing orientations/business models

A business may change its orientation or business model. Facebook changed from a product-orientated business to an advertising business model.

Many car manufacturers now have women on focus groups to influence car design for women drivers. This change was reflected in their business models.

**Now try this**

Initially the budget airline BuzzAir offered an affordable, no-frills service. Passengers could not reserve seats as part of a standard fare. When BuzzAir wanted to increase its number of business passengers, it listened to feedback and now offers a seat reservation option. This has increased sales to its new target market.

(a) State the business orientation and business model BuzzAir initially operated. **(2 marks)**
(b) Describe **one** impact to BuzzAir of changing its business model. **(2 marks)**

# Branding – its importance and dimensions

Branding is important because it makes a business distinctive and memorable. This enables it to stand out from its competitors.

## What are brand dimensions?

These are the components that make the brand distinctive and give it an identity. They make it INSTANTLY RECOGNISABLE and reinforce its IMAGE in the mind of consumers.

**Brand dimensions**

LOGO
A distinct design or lettering

CELEBRITY ENDORSEMENTS
A famous name will increase sales

SYMBOL
An emblem that represents the brand

IMAGES
Give a visual appearance to the brand

COLOURS
Reflect the brand image; make products easy to find

## Brand consistency

All the brand components should reflect the main activity, values and style of the business.

---

## Brand components

Brand components might be: security, fun, safety, luxury, freshness or cleanliness.

A courier company might want a logo or symbol that indicates speed, which might be one of its main brand components.

## Steps in creating a distinctive brand

There are four steps in creating a distinctive brand:

**1** Choose an appropriate name.

**2** Choose a symbol/use logo type (distinctive lettering) for the name.

**3** Decide on brand colours for packaging, posters and stationery.

**4** Have images or endorsements to reinforce the brand identity.

---

## Worked example

Jane and Angelika are setting up a women-only taxi service. They want their brand to reflect their brand components of reliability and safety.

Outline **two** ways in which they can do this. **(2 marks)**

**1** They can choose an appropriate name which shows they are appealing to women, e.g. Hot Pink Wheels.

**2** They can use a logo or symbol to enable passengers to easily recognise their taxis, e.g. a female driver with a female passenger.

If you are asked to 'outline', this means you should provide a broad description without going into detail.

---

## Now try this

Mark has taken over a country pub, The Punchbowl, and wants to show he provides fresh, healthy, local food. He already has a name and a symbol over the door.

Suggest **two** other brand dimensions he can add to reinvent The Punchbowl brand for local people. **(2 marks)**

Remember to think about the components of Mark's brand, such as fresh, healthy food.

# The benefits of building brands

Businesses gain many benefits from building a brand.

## The benefits of branding

- It gives a unique image that potential customers recognise.
- Customers are more willing to try new branded products.
- Customers trust brands, leading to repeat purchases.
- Brands can often charge higher prices.
- It makes a business stand out from its competitors, resulting in increased sales and market share.
- It helps a business to expand its range and increase its profits.

## Brand value

The brand has a monetary value. Anyone who wanted to own that brand would have to pay for the name.

This is because less money needs to be spent on advertising because customers recognise products quickly. They also make repeat purchases and become loyal to a brand.

### Example: Angry Birds

When Angry Birds joined together with Star Wars for a new game, two famous brands were brought together to increase sales.

## Brand personality

People see a brand as having certain characteristics. It may be daring and fun (Go Ape), safe and reliable (HSBC bank) or young and clever (Google, Facebook, Pixar).

The Go Ape brand is seen as daring and fun.

## Brand extension

This means launching a related or adapted product, such as the iPad mini which followed the iPad, or dishwasher tablets which followed Fairy washing-up liquid. As the brand name is known, customers will be more willing to buy.

Dishwasher tablets were a natural brand extension for Fairy.

### Worked example

A well-known confectionery brand is launching its own brand of chewing gum.

**1** What term is used to describe this type of marketing activity?   **(1 mark)**

This is known as brand extension.

**2** Give **one** benefit for brands that do this.   **(1 mark)**

Sales will rise quicker than if this was an unknown brand.

Other correct answers would be:
- Less money is needed to promote the new product because the brand is already known.
- Customers who already like the brand will be eager to try it.

### Now try this

Leaping Lemurs is a video game that many people play on smartphones and tablets. It is a well-known and successful brand that most people have heard of.

Leaping Lemurs has a brand value. Explain **one** reason why this is a benefit to brand owners.   **(2 marks)**

# Market research – types and sources of data

Market research is gathering information about customers, competitors and market trends by collecting PRIMARY and SECONDARY data. This information is used to help a business make decisions. The first step in making these decisions is to obtain relevant data.

## Primary data

- PRIMARY DATA is original data obtained from CUSTOMERS or CONSUMERS.

- Sources include: interviews, questionnaires, analysing sales records, consumer panels and focus/feedback groups.

Questionnaires provide primary data.

## Secondary data

- SECONDARY DATA is data that already EXISTS elsewhere so collecting this is known as DESK RESEARCH.

- Sources include: information in electoral rolls, newspaper reports, trade journals and information stored online.

Written sources, such as books and newspapers, provide secondary data.

## Quantitative data

- QUANTITATIVE DATA is NUMBERS.

- Sources include: sales figures, government statistics and figures produced by research firms, such as Mintel and Keynote.

## Qualitative data

- QUALITATIVE DATA is OPINIONS.

- Sources include: interviews, focus groups and customer surveys asking for views.

## Worked example

Taheer's Garage does MOT testing. He decides to send reminders to all customers who own cars due for testing. He also wants to check how many cars he has tested over the past year.

1 Explain whether Taheer will be obtaining primary or secondary data. **(2 marks)**

Taheer will use primary data because he will be looking for customer names and addresses from his own sales records.

2 Explain whether the data will be quantitative or qualitative. **(2 marks)**

Taheer will be focusing on quantitative data because it is related to the number of customers, not their opinions.

If you are asked to 'explain' then remember to give a reason. Using the word 'because' helps you to link your answer with the reason.

## Now try this

Healthy-care is a well-known high street store selling pharmaceuticals and beauty products. This is a competitive market so keeping customers happy is important to Healthy-care's success. Healthy-care sets up a community panel for invited customers.

(a) What type of data will this provide? **(1 mark)**

(b) Explain **one** way this research can help Healthy-care to improve its products and services. **(2 marks)**

Think about the type of questions Healthy-care might ask its customers and the answers it may get.

# The uses of data to support marketing activity

The aims of the market research will determine the type of data that is collected and used. Qualitative and quantitative data is used for two main reasons:

## ① Understanding trends and making predictions

TRENDS can relate to: market growth or decline, population changes, spending patterns or lifestyle changes.

Identifying and analysing a trend can enable a PREDICTION to be made about the future.

Trends can be analysed to identify areas of growth or decline.

## ② Identifying areas of interest or gaps in the market

AREAS OF INTEREST are products and services customers want to buy or are enquiring about.

A GAP IN THE MARKET is a customer need that is not yet fully met by other businesses. Identifying gaps in the market can provide good ideas for new products, such as the Trunki.

## Marketing activity

The type of marketing activity to be carried out will depend on the results of the market research. This may mean:

- changing or adapting products or services
- offering new or different products
- offering products in new markets.

### Case studies and assessment

In Section B of the assessment there is a detailed case study. The type of business and product/service provided is very important so think about this carefully as you are reading.

This is because the research and marketing activities that are suitable for one type of product may not be suitable for another.

---

### Worked example

A cinema chain wants to increase its mid-week audiences.

**1** Give **two** types of data, one qualitative and one quantitative, that the cinema chain could collect which would provide relevant information. **(2 marks)**

Qualitative data could include asking weekend customers why they do not visit during the week. Quantitative data could be the number of tickets sold at weekdays and weekends over the past year, to identify any trends.

**2** Outline **one** way that this data could be used to support the cinema chain's marketing activities.

**(2 marks)**

The cinema could use this information to see if they should change the prices, times or films shown to attract more people mid-week.

Any suggestions you make **must** be relevant to the **product** or **service**.

### Now try this

A hairdresser, Jo, wants to know if her business would benefit if she closed every Monday and stayed open later at night instead.

**(a)** Give **two** types of data, one qualitative and one quantitative, that she could collect to find out.
**(2 marks)**

**(b)** Describe **two** trends or gaps in the market Jo could identify that would help her. **(4 marks)**

# The uses of internal and external data and situational analysis

INTERNAL data is data held by the business, such as sales figures and customer records. EXTERNAL data is (secondary) data published in reports, newspapers and online. These types of data are used for two main reasons:

## 1 Benchmarking against competitors

BENCHMARKING means checking how the business is performing and comparing with other businesses.

School league tables are a form of benchmarking.

Businesses check and compare product ranges; prices; delivery charges; customer-return policies; and profits, if these are published.

## PESTLE analysis

A PESTLE analysis looks at how outside forces affect the business:

* POLITICAL ISSUES
* ECONOMIC ISSUES
* SOCIAL FACTORS
* TECHNOLOGICAL DEVELOPMENTS
* LEGAL FACTORS
* ENVIRONMENTAL FACTORS.

For further information on PESTLE analysis, go to page 50.

## 2 Producing a situational analysis

SWOT and PESTLE analyses show how the business is performing in the current market.

### SWOT analysis

A SWOT analysis identifies the:

* STRENGTHS and WEAKNESSES in the BUSINESS.
* OPPORTUNITIES and THREATS in the MARKET.

## The use and benefits of situational analysis

SITUATIONAL ANALYSIS is used by a business to look at its own position in the market and assess how it could be affected by trends and developments.

It enables marketing decisions to be made that are based on facts, not guesswork.

It enables the marketing plan to focus on building on strengths, eliminating weaknesses and taking advantage of opportunities.

## Worked example

Mobile phone companies are very competitive.

**1** Identify **three** types of data they may use to benchmark themselves against their competitors.    **(3 marks)**

They will compare the range of handsets they have on offer, the features of these and the prices they charge.

**2** Give **one** benefit they may gain by carrying out a SWOT analysis.    **(1 mark)**

They can identify any weaknesses in their provision and try to eliminate these to increase sales.

Remember to consider the type of business model carefully when considering the types of data you choose.

## Now try this

Always make sure you read the scenario of each question carefully.

Harry has a fitness club that is doing well. He decides to expand and open two more clubs in other towns.

Outline **two** risks of doing this without carrying out a situational analysis.    **(4 marks)**

# The purpose of market research and analysis

Market research data is always collected and analysed for a reason. Here are four different reasons for collecting and analysing market research data:

## 1 To identify TARGET MARKETS

This is the market the business aims to supply by finding a gap in what is currently offered.

- A MARKET SEGMENT is a group of customers in a market who have similar characteristics and needs.
- Many businesses build a profile of the TARGET CUSTOMER – their age, income, lifestyle, location and what products they use now.

## 2 To identify COMPETITOR ACTIVITY

This can be done by checking their websites, visiting their premises, reading press reports and talking to customers to:

- summarise the KEY POINTS – location, price, quality, range, service
- identify their STRENGTHS and WEAKNESSES from a customer's point of view.

## 3 To understand CONSUMER BEHAVIOUR

Knowing why consumers make a purchase means the business knows how to appeal to them.

- The business needs to identify: customer needs and wants, how much they spend, what else they buy and what they ignore or dislike.
- Methods include: focus groups, customer panels, mystery shoppers, observing customers, surveys, analysing customer data and published reports.

Focus groups are a good way of understanding customer needs.

## 4 To identify MARKET TRENDS

Key factors are:

- Market size and value of sales revenue (How big is it? Can we make a profit?)
- Market growth rate (How fast/slow?)
- The level of competition (Is it cut-throat? Can we survive?)
- The number of products already in the market (Is ours any different?).

> Identifying the target market also means that in-depth research can focus on this particular type of customer.

### Worked example

Identify **two** benefits to a business of identifying its target market and profiling its target customers. **(2 marks)**

1 The product or service offered can be tailored to meet the needs of those customers.

2 Promotions and advertisements can be targeted at specific groups.

### Now try this

Martin spent four years selling cars. He now wants to open his own car showroom and specialise in selling sports cars.

(a) Identify **two** ways he can find out about the behaviour of his potential new customers.
**(2 marks)**

(b) Explain **one** way that carrying out research on his target market will help to improve his business.
**(2 marks)**

# Interpreting key market research findings

Research findings can provide information on MARKET SIZE, MARKET GROWTH and MARKET SHARE.

## Market size

This can be calculated in different ways:

- by VALUE – for example, total sales in the UK
- by BRAND – which are the most popular?
- by TYPE OF CUSTOMER – for example, spending habits vary between men and women and between different age groups.

## Market share

This is usually calculated as a percentage of sales of product by one company and shows the popularity of a particular product.

In a MASS market, such as the groceries market, large firms (e.g. Tesco and Sainsbury's) want a HIGH market share, so they can squeeze small firms out.

Small firms do better if they focus on a NICHE market, e.g. farm shops or ethnic foods. They often settle for a LOWER market share.

Organic baby food is a niche market product.

## Market growth

Market growth means the market is worth more each year.

Markets can GROW or DECLINE – and at different rates.

Markets can be:

- FAST GROWING = opportunities for high sales/profits; more competition from large firms. Price is important.
- SLOW GROWING = fewer threats from competitors; no immediate reward; products evolve based on feedback and new technology. Quality is important.

### Benefits of a lower market share

Operating in a niche market means:

- products can be sold at premium prices
- the business is not a threat to large firms
- the business can target its advertising and promotion to its target market
- expenses related to operating large premises/expansion are avoided.

## Worked example

Joel wants to open a cycle shop. He reads that the UK bicycle market was valued at £700m in 2012 and is forecast to be worth £800m in 2016.

Use this information about market size and growth to discuss his decision.   **(4 marks)**

The bicycle market is large and sales are high. It is steadily growing so Joel's business will have a good chance of success. However, large firms may dominate the mass market so Joel may be better focusing on a niche market selling mountain bikes or bike accessories.

'Evaluating' means identifying the points for and against an idea and coming to a realistic conclusion based on this information. These questions gain the most marks. Identify positive reasons and negative reasons, and give a reasoned conclusion.

## Now try this

Referring back to the worked example, Joel reads that twice as many men cycle as women. He is now wondering whether to sell expensive designer cycle clothes for men.

Evaluate this idea.   **(8 marks)**

# PESTLE analysis

A PESTLE analysis involves researching data about the wider environment to identify issues that might affect the business. A PESTLE analysis highlights important aspects that will affect the business. This includes both threats and opportunities for the business.

POLITICAL ISSUES –
Government policies and
spending plans

ENVIRONMENTAL
FACTORS – laws on pollution and
'green' issues and concerns

ECONOMIC ISSUES –
factors that affect consumer
spending, (e.g. unemployment or
tax increases)

**PESTLE**

LEGAL FACTORS –
related legislation or regulations
(e.g. employment legislation)

SOCIAL ISSUES –
changing lifestyles,
attitudes and spending
habits (e.g. decreasing
birth rate)

TECHNOLOGICAL
DEVELOPMENTS –
new innovations and
inventions (e.g. WiFi)

## Worked example

Joel, who wants to open a cycle shop (see page 49), has read in the news that wages are rising and consumer spending is increasing. In the same paper, it said that the government wants to build more cycle lanes to encourage more people to cycle to help reduce rising obesity levels and cut down fuel emissions in cities. The government may also make it compulsory to wear a cycle helmet to help reduce the number of serious injuries, even though people don't like wearing cycle helmets. Joel is now keen to open a bicycle shop, selling the latest light, aerodynamic racing bikes.

Carry out a PESTLE analysis for him using this information.
**(6 marks)**

A PESTLE analysis for Joel identifies the following relevant issues:

POLITICAL – the government is spending money on building more cycle lanes. It wants fewer people to be overweight.

ECONOMIC – wages are rising and consumer spending is increasing.

SOCIAL – more people are overweight.

TECHNOLOGY – improvements have enabled lighter bikes to be made and racing bikes to go faster.

LEGAL – it may soon be compulsory to wear a cycle helmet.

ENVIRONMENTAL – bikes do not pollute the environment.

Read this case study carefully to identify relevant information for each PESTLE area. You don't need to complete this in a certain order. Do the most obvious ones first!

Evaluate his idea by identifying arguments in favour and arguments against and then come to a conclusion. Think carefully about who Joel's target customer would be.

## Now try this

Use the information you know about the cycling market (see page 49) and the information given in the PESTLE analysis (in the worked example) to evaluate Joel's idea to open a shop in a niche market, selling racing bikes.
**(8 marks)**

# The marketing mix – an overview

The marketing mix is all the factors a business must consider to sell its products successfully to its target customer.

## The 4 Ps

The marketing mix is often called the '4 Ps', because each factor starts with 'P'.

It is important that all aspects of the marketing mix complement each other and work together well. Just like baking a cake, it is important to get the right balance of ingredients. The 'mix' must be appropriate for that business.

### 1 Price

The PRICE gives customers an indication of quality. In a competitive market changes in the price can affect demand.

   = Revenue

### 3 Place

PLACE means having the product available to customers in the right place at the right time and in premium condition.

A business may sell DIRECT to customers or through a DISTRIBUTION CHANNEL (for example, through a retailer or wholesaler).

Keeping goods fresh and in premium condition is very important.

### 2 Product

The PRODUCT must meet the needs of the customer. Products targeted at the business market may need to be different from those targeted at consumers.

The term 'product' includes the brand name, the range offered, the materials used and the packaging.

### 4 Promotion

PROMOTION is the way a business makes potential customers aware of its products.

The aim is to create awareness, communicate benefits and features, build the brand image and boost sales, for example, through social media.

Social media is used by many businesses to promote their products.

## Worked example

HSL Food provides catering packs of soups and sauces for restaurants.

Identify **two** ways in which its marketing mix will differ from a business selling soup to consumers. **(2 marks)**

1 Product – HSL will sell its products in bulk and its catering packs will be much larger than packs for consumers.

2 Place – HSL will sell through wholesalers or direct to caterers. If it was selling to consumers, it would sell through retailers.

## Now try this

Explain **one** reason why place is an important aspect of the marketing mix. **(2 marks)**

 You could also say that the price for caterers would probably include a discount. Promotion will be through sales reps rather than on TV or in the press.

# Product differentiation

A business must decide what products to produce and how to DIFFERENTIATE these from others on the market.

## Core and augmented products

- The CORE PRODUCT is the basic item offered, such as a TV.

- An AUGMENTED PRODUCT has 'extras' that make it more desirable, such as a 3D TV sold with a guarantee.

A 3D TV is an example of an augmented product.

## Unique selling point (USP)

This is the key aspect of the product that makes it DIFFERENT or SPECIAL.

It sets the product apart from its competitors – for example, a new and improved processor in a smartphone.

A new, faster processor is an example of a USP for a smartphone.

## Extra benefits

Additional benefits also augment the product and add to its USP. These include:

- free delivery
- order tracking
- excellent customer service
- gift wrapping
- price matching
- a 'no-quibble' returns policy.

## Why differentiate?

Businesses need to differentiate their product or service to:

- avoid the risk of failure
- attract customers
- demonstrate their product meets customer needs
- stand out from their competitors.

## Worked example

T4U is an online T-shirt business that prints unisex T-shirts. It specialises in printing novelty and personalised designs.

**1** Identify the USP of T4U.    **(1 mark)**

T4U makes and prints customised unisex T-shirts so a customer can suggest a design and wording.

**2** Outline **two** ways T4U could augment their product to increase sales.    **(2 marks)**

T4U could offer gift boxes for T-shirts given as presents. They could also offer one free T-shirt in every pack of ten, to encourage group orders.

## Now try this

A company has produced a brand of cotton baby suits with enhanced grip to make it easier for babies to crawl.

Explain how this feature should increase sales.    **(2 marks)**

There are several acceptable answers to question 2. Think about the extras that would attract you if you were buying from them. Their aim is to stand out from the competition.

# Product life cycle

Each product has a life cycle. This can be long (a children's book) or short (fashion shoes). Products at the end of their life cycle need rejuvenating or replacing.

Businesses should know where each of their products or services is positioned within the life cycle. At the saturation stage, before products enter the decline stage, they may decide on an EXTENSION STRATEGY.

The product is launched/released onto the market.

If the launch is successful, sales increase sharply and the product may make a profit for the first time.

Sales growth slows down, but repeat customers continue to buy and customers become loyal. The market becomes saturated as rivals bring out competing products.

Eventually the product is outdated and there is a big fall in sales, leading to withdrawl.

SALES

| Development/ Introduction | Growth | Maturity | Decline |

SALES

TIME

What questions should businesses ask at each stage?

| What promotion methods will encourage customers to trial a product? | How can we meet demand and maintain customer service? | How can we encourage repeat purchases and build customer loyalty? | How can we innovate products to compete with competitors? Should we use extension strategies? |

## Extension strategies

Extension strategies are ways of increasing the shelf life of a product. They involve changing the product slightly so it has a fresh appeal to the target market or so it appeals to a new market.

LEGO's Friends range is designed to appeal to girls and is an example of an extension strategy.

## Selling in new markets

Selling in NEW MARKETS is another way of extending the life cycle of a product. This may mean selling overseas or to a new segment of an existing market. For example, a men's barber shop could widen its market by converting to a unisex hair salon.

SATURATION is the stage between MATURITY and DECLINE. It is the stage when every customer likely to buy a product or service has done so; the market has become saturated.

## Worked example

A cereal manufacturer is concerned because sales of one product, Breakabix, are falling.

Identify **two** possible extension strategies that the company could use. **(2 marks)**

1 The cereal manufacturer could create new packaging to make the product look more modern and attractive.

2 The manufacturer could improve or change the product by adding new flavours or varieties.

## Now try this

1 Identify the stage of the product life cycle where sales are likely to be rising most rapidly. **(1 mark)**

2 Explain **one** reason why a business might use an extension strategy in the maturity stage of a product. **(2 marks)**

Other extension strategies include: lowering the price, increasing advertising, giving free gifts or other promotional offers.

# Product portfolios

The PRODUCT PORTFOLIO is the range of products produced by the business.

## Product mix

The PRODUCT MIX is the variety of products offered.

- Some firms concentrate on ONE TYPE of product and offer a RANGE of items. For example, Patak makes a range of Indian foods.

- Others make a wide VARIETY of products. For example, Samsung makes home appliances, smartphones, netbooks and TVs.

## Product portfolio analysis

The business has to decide:

- how many different products to make
- which products to launch and when
- when to withdraw a product
- which products are doing well or badly now and which may do well or badly in the future
- how to increase sales.

Many electronics firms have a broad portfolio.

## Benefits of maintaining a broad portfolio

- ✓ It reduces risk – some products will sell well.
- ✓ It appeals to different customer segments.
- ✓ It increases revenue.
- ✓ Declining products are replaced and have less impact on sales revenue.
- ✓ All products may have the same USP, which consolidates the brand.

## Disadvantages of maintaining a broad portfolio

- ✗ It costs money to develop, launch and stock new products.
- ✗ A wide range may confuse customers.
- ✗ More space is needed for storage.
- ✗ Some products may not be profitable.
- ✗ Attention may be taken away from the most profitable products.

### Worked example

Give **two** reasons why a business should review its product portfolio regularly.    **(2 marks)**

1 Some products may be doing well and others may not. If a product is unprofitable, it may have to be withdrawn.

2 Some products may be in decline and need to be revamped in some way and relaunched or withdrawn from the market.

To answer this, think how you would react if you saw that there was a shampoo or a yoghurt called Domestos or Dettol!

### Now try this

Explain **one** reason why the products in a portfolio should complement each other and fit with the image and focus of the business.

**(2 marks)**

Think about the product life cycle when you are answering questions about a product portfolio.

# Pricing strategies

A pricing strategy is the method used to determine what price to charge. There are four main methods depending on the product and the level of competition. All methods have advantages and disadvantages.

## 1 Focus on costs

- COST PLUS PRICING: this is the cost of making the product + a percentage of profit.
- MARK UP PRICING: this is the cost of making the product + a percentage mark up (i.e. a percentage of the cost of making).

✓ Advantage: easy to calculate and costs are covered.

✗ Disadvantage: if customers would be happy to pay more for the product then revenue is lost.

## 2 Focus on a competitive market

- COMPETITIVE PRICING: using a similar price to competitors.
- PRICE TAKING: using exactly the same price as competitors.

✓ Advantage: stops sales being lost to competitors.

✗ Disadvantage: does not allow for extras that customers may be prepared to pay for.

## 3 Focus on asking a high price

- SKIMMING: asking a high price at the launch of a new/novelty product.
- PREMIUM PRICING: asking a high price for a desirable, luxury product.

Designer handbags are sold at premium prices.

 Advantages: maximises profits which helps repay development costs; boosts brand image.

✗ Disadvantages: customers may wait until the price falls or buy from competitors; sales may be low.

## 4 Focus on asking a low price

PENETRATION PRICING: asking a low price at the launch of the product to interest people.

✓ Advantages: gains interest and boosts sales; encourages customer/brand loyalty.

✗ Disadvantages: may mean low profit/selling at a loss; sales may fall when price increases; customers may think that the product is poor quality.

New brands of chocolate and sweets are often launched at a lower price.

## Worked example

Matthias repairs car bodywork. He is starting his own business and cannot decide whether to charge a low or a high price.

Give **one** benefit for each choice. **(2 marks)**

A low price means he will not lose business to competitors. A high price may mean less revenue at the start but if he offers value for money then satisfied customers will recommend him to others.

## Now try this

Rob is updating his bathroom. He sees a discounted bathroom suite in a DIY store and then decides to buy expensive Italian tiles. His plumber says the work will take a week and quotes him a fixed price for the job.

Describe the **three** different pricing strategies he has experienced. **(6 marks)**

Give a **reason** for your choice in each case.

# Elasticity of demand

Elasticity of demand is the degree to which demand (and sales) increase as prices fall – and vice versa.

## Understanding demand

DEMAND normally INCREASES when prices FALL. It DECREASES when prices RISE.

If it changes a lot, demand is ELASTIC. This means prices increase but the item is non-essential.

If demand changes very little, it is INELASTIC. This means prices increase but the item is essential.

Demand for electricity is inelastic. We still need power, even when prices rise.

## Price elasticity of demand (PED)

This is calculated with this formula:

$$PED = \frac{\% \text{ change in quantity demanded}}{\% \text{ change in price}}$$

PED which is >1 is elastic.
PED which is <1 is inelastic.

Demand for strawberries is elastic. If prices rise, we buy something else.

## Why calculate price elasticity of demand (PED)?

Calculating PED means a business knows which product sales will fall a lot if prices are increased and which will fall very little.

It can then change prices only on those items that would still be purchased.

One exception to the law of demand is luxury goods. Sales may increase as prices rise!

## Working it out

Stationery shop owner Ken increased prices by 10 per cent. Sales of envelopes fell by 20 per cent. Sales of paper fell by 5 per cent.

Envelopes are ELASTIC because sales fell by more than the price rise.
PED is 20/10 = 2. So, >1.

Paper is INELASTIC because sales fell by LESS than the price rise.
PED is 5/10 = 0.5. So, <1.

## Worked example

Explain **one** way elasticity of demand can affect pricing decisions in a business.     **(2 marks)**

The price elasticity of demand shows how much demand will fall if prices are increased and vice versa. All products have a different PED and this can be calculated using a formula. If a product is elastic then demand will fall quickly if prices are increased. This means it is better for business revenue if price rises are restricted to inelastic goods.

The main point is to remember the benefits of calculating PED for a business.

## Now try this

Refer back to the Working it out box and explain **two** actions Ken, the stationery shop owner, should take to make sure his sales don't fall.
**(4 marks)**

# Place – distribution channels

The aim of DISTRIBUTION is to get the product to the target customer in the right condition and at the right time.

## Distribution channels

A DISTRIBUTION CHANNEL is the method used to get the product from the producer to the consumer. It can be DIRECT to the consumer or INDIRECT via a wholesaler or distributor. The best channel(s) for a product will depend on the type of product and the buying habits of the target customer.

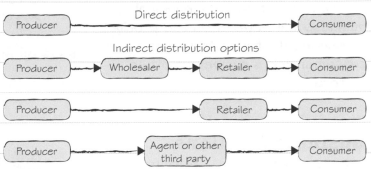

The different distribution channels that can be used by businesses.

## Within the market

The positioning of the product (or where goods are sold) within the market depends on the product being sold. Some products are more suitable for DIRECT SELLING than others, for example fresh foods and craft items at farmers' markets and fêtes.

- Low-cost items, such as sweets, are sold by shops and stores.
- Luxury goods are sold in high-end stores.
- Specialist goods (for example, sportswear) have their own outlets.

## Direct and indirect distribution channels

DIRECT CHANNELS include:

- online sales
- factory shops
- farm shops.

INDIRECT CHANNELS include:

- WHOLESALERS who buy mass-produced goods in bulk and sell them on in smaller quantities
- PRODUCERS, such as Heinz, who sell to large retailers like Tesco
- other THIRD PARTIES, including agents, concessions and TV shopping channels.

## Worked example

Outline **one** reason why manufacturers, such as Coca Cola and Pepsi, do not use direct distribution methods. **(1 mark)**

These manufacturers make vast quantities of drinks and want to sell them in much larger quantities than private individuals would buy. It is more cost-effective to deal with large retail firms or wholesalers rather than lots of individuals.

With direct channels there is **no** intermediary so prices should be cheaper.

## Now try this

An online kitchenware business decides to increase its sales by recruiting reps who go from door to door with catalogues. It also opens stores in two large towns.

Identify **three** distribution channels it uses.

**(3 marks)**

# Place – business location

Physical businesses have to choose their location carefully.

## Factors influencing business location

The right location for a physical business will depend on the product or service it offers, its target customer and a number of other factors.

Nearness to customers

Access to suppliers

Transport links

**Where to locate?**

Price of land/ premises

Communications

Location of competitors

Availability of labour

## Business locations

- Those selling to the PUBLIC need to attract passing trade (for example, with nearby parking). They need to locate near similar businesses (for example, in retail parks, shopping malls, town centres).

- Those selling to BUSINESS BUYERS are often located in out-of-town business parks or enterprise areas.

- ECOMMERCE BUSINESSES that sell goods only online can be located anywhere with good transport and communication links. Look at page 62 for more information.

Nearby parking increases trade for retailers.

## Selling through multiple channels

Many businesses use multiple channels, for example Fat Face sells clothes online, in stores and in catalogues. ALL channels must be appropriate to the product, target customers and size of business.

## Worked example

Describe **two** factors that would influence the location of a convenience store.
**(4 marks)**

**1** The store owner will want to be in a neighbourhood with a busy local community because these people will be the main customers.

**2** Passing trade and good access for customers are essential, so a shop on a main road with lots of parking would be ideal.

**Both** the location and the distribution channels used **must** fit with the product, the target customer and the size of business.

## Now try this

A jeweller moves premises from a shopping mall to a side street when business rents rise.

Give **one** reason why sales are likely to fall as a result. **(1 mark)**

The best place to locate a business is the cheapest possible place where you will still attract your target customers.

# The promotional mix, budget and channels

The PROMOTIONAL MIX is the combination of methods chosen to advertise and promote a product or brand. The best mix will depend on the product, target customer, competitors and budget.

PUBLIC RELATIONS AND PUBLICITY
(News stories, feature articles, sponsorship)

PERSONAL SELLING
(Trade fairs, exhibitions, sales reps)

EMARKETING
(Text messages, internet adverts, social media, blogs, search engine optimisation)

**Promotional channels**

SALES PROMOTIONS
(Vouchers, coupons, competitions, point-of-sale materials, free gifts)

DIRECT MARKETING
(Mailshots, email newsletters, flyers)

ADVERTISING
(TV, radio, cinema, press, posters)

## The promotional budget

The PROMOTIONAL BUDGET is the amount of money that can be spent on promotions. Some methods are expensive (for example, TV advertising) while others are cheap or even free (email newsletters or celebrity endorsements).

All methods used must be assessed to see which ones increase sales revenue the most.

Top $14.95

## 'Above the line' or 'below the line' promotions?

ABOVE THE LINE = paid-for promotions: TV, radio, cinema, press, Google pay-per-click

BELOW THE LINE = all other types of promotion: sales promotions, mailshots, email newsletters, press features, celebrity endorsements, telesales, personal selling

A celebrity endorsement is free but many celebrities are paid to sponsor a product.

## Worked example

Give **two** benefits to a small clothes retailer of using 'below the line' promotions.    **(4 marks)**

1 Below the line promotions cost less than above the line advertisements and some are free.

2 Unlike large firms, a small business will not need to advertise on TV, or even in the press, and can inform customers of new stock by email or post very cheaply.

## Now try this

Describe **two** ways that a business can assess the effectiveness of an advertisement that it places in a magazine.    **(4 marks)**

Think about how the business can tempt customers to respond to them directly or give them information after reading the advert.

Always think about the behaviour of the target customer. What TV channels do they watch? What newspapers or magazines do they read? Do they use social media?

# Viral marketing and guerrilla advertising

Viral marketing means encouraging people to tell their online contacts about your product. This spreads information for free. This can be done using any type of social media, such as websites, blogs and other online platforms, that enables users to post and share information.

## Facebook

Having a Facebook page and encouraging people to subscribe to the newsfeed means people can 'Like' and 'Share' information about the business with their contacts.

Some firms offer financial rewards for sharing a page (for example, makers of online games).

## Twitter

Having a Twitter feed enables a business to promote new products and services to its followers, who may retweet it to others. The Twitter hashtag can be used to promote a product, event or new idea.

## YouTube

Posting videos to show a product or service in an original way not always associated with it is done by many large businesses. This can quickly go viral if it is novel enough. Take a look at T-Mobile's parody Royal Wedding video, posted in April 2011. Tying in with their slogan 'life's for sharing' it has had some 27 million views.

## Guerrilla advertising

These are unconventional tactics used to promote a brand, product or idea – for example, a flash mob, a midnight walk, graffiti, street art or an unusual display. It should be original so people want to share it online.

## Worked example

Describe **two** benefits of using social media to carry out viral marketing.

**(4 marks)**

1 Social media enables a business to promote its brand or new products and, if the theme or message is interesting, novel or funny, then people will pass it on.
2 Using social media to promote a new idea or product is cheaper than traditional advertising, which means wider publicity can be obtained very cheaply.

Social media also lets businesses monitor what people are saying about them – and respond promptly to negative feedback. This can turn a disaster into a triumph!

## Now try this

Mark has created a new app that monitors people's pulse rate when they are exercising.

Describe **one** way he could use guerrilla advertising to carry out viral marketing.

**(2 marks)**

The aim will be to have a novel (and cheap) tactic that will go viral. Do you have any good ideas?

# Consistency and the marketing mix

The elements of the marketing mix must be CONSISTENT so that customers always receive the same message about the product or brand. This message depends on the desired brand image and the target customer.

## 1 Price

- Mass-market budget products are priced cheaply and competitively.
- High-end luxury goods firms often use a premium pricing strategy.

## 2 Product

- Mass-market budget products are designed to be used and thrown away. Most are made as cheaply as possible.
- High-end luxury products and designer goods are designed to be used again and again. They are made from quality materials.

## 3 Place

- Mass-market budget goods are sold in markets, pound shops and discount stores. Displays will be basic.
- High-end luxury items are sold in department stores, city centres and shopping malls. Displays will be spacious and well lit.

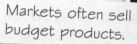

Markets often sell budget products.

## 4 Promotion

- Budget items are promoted through leaflet drops and door-to-door sales or point-of-sale materials in store.
- Mass-produced goods are advertised on national television.
- High-end luxury goods are advertised on posters, in newspapers and glossy magazines.

Point-of-sale material is used to promote budget items.

## Worked example

A toy shop wants to give the image of being young at heart while also caring about the welfare of its young customers.

Suggest **two** ways that its marketing mix can reflect this. **(4 marks)**

**1** The shop should stock products that are fun to use, but should also include some that are educational. All products should be safe, reliable and well made.

**2** Products should be available at a range of prices so that no child is disadvantaged because their parents cannot afford more expensive toys. Prices should be competitive so that parents think the store provides good value for money.

## Now try this

Stylewise is a high-street clothing store that sells a range of cheap clothing, including items replicated from the runway, for a target market of young men and women.

Explain **one** reason why Stylewise's marketing mix is consistent. **(2 marks)**

Answer this question by identifying its target customers and explain how its marketing mix reinforces its brand image.

You could suggest that the shop would be in a busy shopping centre and so some stock would be displayed for children to touch or use.

Promotions could include staff demonstrations of the toys and colourful leaflets illustrating the items stocked.

# Ebusiness and ecommerce

There is an important difference between the terms EBUSINESS and ECOMMERCE.

## What is ebusiness?

Ebusiness means that many of the business' operations; such as stock control, financial systems, human resources and customer relations, are linked by technology.

Computerised stock control is one aspect of an ebusiness.

## What is ecommerce?

Ecommerce means the business buys and/or sells goods over the internet. It may also offer customer service online.

Croft Mill, an online fabric business, is an example of an ecommerce business.

## Benefits of ebusiness

- ✓ Saves money and time as all activities are linked – for example, sales and stock control.
- ✓ The business can respond promptly to enquiries and orders.
- ✓ Staff are more efficient as they have more information at their fingertips.
- ✓ Customer records can be analysed.
- ✓ Customers can be sent targeted emails.
- ✓ Financial transactions, marketing and sales campaigns can be analysed.

## Benefits of ecommerce

- ✓ The business can sell goods 24/7.
- ✓ It is cheaper than having retail premises.
- ✓ More orders can be processed.
- ✓ Products can be promoted and sold in overseas markets.
- ✓ The business can sell through mobile sites and apps on smartphones and tablets.
- ✓ It can promote products using social media and provide direct links to allow online purchase.

## Worked example

Desiree buys goods online and at car boot sales. She sells them from her eBay shop.

Identify whether Desiree runs an ebusiness or whether she is using ecommerce to make her living. **(1 mark)**

Desiree uses ecommerce to make her living because she buys and sells items online. She does not have other business operations linked by technology.

To answer this question you need to know the difference between ebusiness and ecommerce.

Use the number of possible marks to guide you on the length of your answer and how much detail is needed.

## Now try this

An ebusiness has its stock control system linked to its product database and its website. This means that customers can see immediately if products are out of stock.

Explain **two** benefits of this system to the business and its customers. **(4 marks)**

# Influences on the marketing mix

All businesses should regularly identify key areas of influence on their marketing mix. This is better than reacting only when there is a crisis.

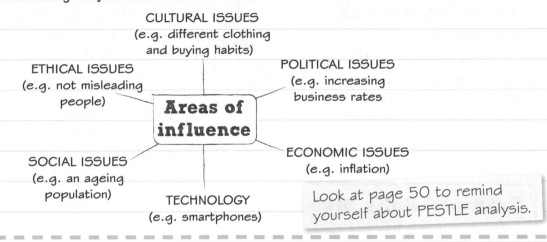

CULTURAL ISSUES
(e.g. different clothing and buying habits)

ETHICAL ISSUES
(e.g. not misleading people)

POLITICAL ISSUES
(e.g. increasing business rates)

**Areas of influence**

SOCIAL ISSUES
(e.g. an ageing population)

ECONOMIC ISSUES
(e.g. inflation)

TECHNOLOGY
(e.g. smartphones)

Look at page 50 to remind yourself about PESTLE analysis.

## Environmental and legal issues

Businesses that undertake a PESTLE analysis will also check:

- environmental issues (such as packaging)
- legal issues (such as changes to consumer laws).

## Possible effects

The key areas of influence shown above can affect ALL parts of the marketing mix in one way or another:

- PRODUCT – may need updating because of technological changes
- PRICE – may need lowering if incomes are falling
- PLACE – may need to change if rates increase
- PROMOTION – may now be more effective online rather than advertising in the press.

## Worked example

A UK clothing store decides to open branches in other countries in Europe and in Asia.

What factors will it need to consider in relation to any **two** aspects of its marketing mix? **(2 marks)**

1 Product – the stock may need changing because of different styles, climate and/or cultural differences.

2 Price – buyers may have less money to spend and competition from established firms may be strong so prices may need to be reduced.

Other suggestions:
Place – because buying habits will be different, the type of location and layout may need to change.
Promotion – these would be different because of language issues and cultural differences.

This task tests your ability to read and understand a case study – which you will have to do in the assessment test.

## Now try this

To maintain its market share, the technology company Techsmart tries to produce technology that fulfils a customer need. They recently introduced a new fingerprint sensor on their new smartphone which identifies the owner, so no password is needed. It also launched a new range of smartphones which are sold at a lower price, mainly to attract buyers in developing markets.

Use this information to describe **two** key influences on Techsmart's marketing mix.

**(4 marks)**

# Evaluating the effectiveness of the marketing mix

If the marketing mix is effective, sales and profits should increase.

## Assessing SMART objectives

Checking whether SMART objectives have been achieved shows areas that are doing well and also shows those which could be improved.

## Reviewing the marketing mix

If some objectives are not being met, one or more of the 4 'Ps' – PRODUCT, PRICE, PLACE or PROMOTION – may need to be adjusted.

The marketing mix must be effective for the target to be achieved.

## Example: Bob's Bike Shop

Bob's bike shop has the target of selling 10 bikes each week.

If Bob's target is SMART (SPECIFIC, MEASURABLE, ACHIEVABLE, REALISTIC, TIME-BASED), but he regularly fails to meet this target, then his marketing mix needs to be adapted.

## Questions Bob should ask:

* PRODUCT – Am I stocking the right products for my target customer?
* PRICE – Am I selling them at the best price compared with my competitors?
* PLACE – Is my shop in the right area, are my stock levels too low so sales fall through?
* PROMOTION – Do people know my shop exists and what type of bikes I sell?

### Worked example

A fitness club set a target of gaining 200 new members in six months. They only gained 120.

Describe **one** action the club now needs to take.          **(2 marks)**

The club should review its target to see if this was SMART; namely, if it was achievable and realistic in that length of time. If this was the case, the club should review each aspect of the marketing mix to see how this could be changed to enable the next target to be met.

If you are reviewing SMART targets or a marketing mix in the assessment test, make sure that your suggestions are relevant to the case study you are given and the type of business being discussed.

### Now try this

Explain the link between setting SMART objectives and reviewing the marketing mix.          **(2 marks)**

# Exam skills 1

You will have 1 hour 30 minutes to answer the written test. There are 50 marks. The paper is in two parts: Section A and Section B. Section A has mainly individual questions. Section B will have questions based around a case study that will start the section. There will be questions on all the learning aims: A, B and C.

## Important features of the test

- The test is in two sections: A and B.
- You should answer ALL the questions using black ink or ballpoint pen.
- Spaces are provided for your answers.
- The marks for each question are shown in brackets.

You will find a highlighter useful, to highlight command words and key terms in the questions, as well as rough paper for notes.

## General hints and tips

✓ Write neatly and clearly.
✓ Do not worry if you do not use all the space allowed for your answer.
✓ Use the marks to guide you on how long to spend on a question and how detailed the answer should be.
✓ Allow time at the end to check through your work.

## Command words

These tell you how to write your answer:

- 'Name', 'State', 'Give', 'Identify', 'Outline' mean give a brief, precise response without going into detail.
- 'Explain' and 'Describe' mean a reason is needed for the answer given.
- 'Evaluate' means reviewing the information, giving advantages and disadvantages and then forming a realistic conclusion.
- 'Assess' and 'Analyse' mean that you need to look closely at all the factors that apply and consider their importance.
- 'Discuss' means thinking about all the aspects of a topic and why they are important.

## Preparing for the test

✓ Revise the key marketing terms and meanings you need to know.
✓ Check that you can define and explain these terms.
✓ Arrive in good time for the test.
✓ If you feel panicky, read through a few questions at the start.

If you have any sort of problem during the test (e.g. your pen stops working), tell the invigilator immediately.

## Worked example

If you are given a business context, make sure your answer is relevant to it.

Sundown Farm is organising its annual music festival and has to decide how to sell the tickets.

Outline **one** direct distribution channel and **one** indirect distribution channel that it could use.        **(2 marks)**

This question tests whether you know about different channels of distribution. These can be direct or indirect (through a retailer, wholesaler or agent).

Sundown Farm could sell the tickets direct to consumers from its own website. This is a direct channel of distribution because the farm deals direct with consumers. Or it could use a ticket agency to sell the tickets on its behalf. This is an indirect channel because it involves someone else.

If you had to describe the advantages and disadvantages of each channel, what would you say?

# Exam skills 2

The assessment test is in two sections: A and B.

## Sections A and B

- In Section A, a FEW questions may be based on a short case study.
- In Section B, ALL the questions are based on a more detailed case study.
- A CASE STUDY is a scenario relating to a specific business.
- You should expect to spend longer on Section B.

## Hints and tips

- You can do the questions in any order. If one puzzles you, leave it and carry on.
- Aim to do one section at a time. Once you start thinking about the case study in Section B, you are better to continue focusing on this.
- You do NOT lose marks for a wrong answer, so your best guess is better than leaving a blank space.
- Use the marks given for a question to guide you on your answer. If you are asked for two points and you only give one, you cannot get full marks.

## Marketing terms to revise

- ✓ Target customer and target market
- ✓ SMART and corporate objectives
- ✓ Business orientation
- ✓ Market share and market trends
- ✓ The marketing mix
- ✓ USP and brand image
- ✓ Product life cycle and extension strategy
- ✓ Product portfolio
- ✓ Pricing strategies
- ✓ Distribution channels
- ✓ Promotional mix

## Check you know the difference between:

- ✓ B2B and B2C
- ✓ Customer and consumer
- ✓ Goods and services markets
- ✓ Capital and consumer goods markets
- ✓ Niche and mass markets
- ✓ SWOT and PESTLE analyses
- ✓ Primary and secondary data
- ✓ Quantitative and qualitative data
- ✓ Core and augmented products
- ✓ Ebusiness and ecommerce
- ✓ Above the line and below the line promotions

## Worked example

Fashionista, a high street clothing chain, is carrying out market research to find out more about their customers and their spending patterns.

Outline **two** benefits of doing this.          **(2 marks)**

1  Fashionista will learn more about its target customers, how much customers spend in stores and which lines are the most/least popular.

2  Fashionista can use this information to stock the lines its customers want to buy at prices they can afford.

Read the context carefully. This is a high street chain so it will have shops all over the country.

A major benefit of market research is the information it provides.

The business then needs to use this information to improve sales.

# Exam skills 3

You will improve your chances if you make sure that you have revised all the key areas that are likely to be covered.

## Revision topics

Before the test make sure you know:

- ✓ the difference between key terms, for example B2B and B2C, niche and mass markets, quantitative and qualitative data, ebusiness and ecommerce

- ✓ the importance and benefits of marketing to business and how it is used by businesses

- ✓ the benefits of distinctive branding and dimensions of a brand

- ✓ the use and purpose of market research in business

- ✓ the marketing mix, including product portfolios, pricing strategies, promotional mix and distribution strategies

- ✓ about competitors, customer behaviour and other factors that affect the market for a product

- ✓ the factors that influence the marketing mix

- ✓ how to evaluate the marketing mix.

## More about evaluation

'Evaluation' and 'Discussion' questions are usually worth the most marks.

- To 'evaluate' you have to identify the plus and minus points. Jot these down in two columns, aim for a similar number in each.

- To 'discuss' you have to think about how the points interrelate. You could mind map each point.

- For both types of question give a sensible conclusion you can justify for that business, based on the points you have made.

### More tips about the case study

- ✓ Read it carefully, then re-read it.

- ✓ Imagine it is your business and any problems are yours too.

- ✓ Link the theory you know to different aspects of the business – for example, brand, price, distribution, promotion.

- ✓ Read each question carefully. Then answer each one using the correct marketing terms whenever you can.

## Worked example

Lottie is starting a dog-walking business. Evaluate her idea of promoting it using social media. **(8 marks)**

Start by thinking about the target customer for this business.

Social media means using social networking services such as Facebook and Twitter to promote the business. The advantages are that customers or other people who read about it can share this information with their friends. This costs nothing. Something really interesting could even go viral so lots of people read it.

Defining social media tells the examiner you know what this means.

Explain the advantages and how Lottie's business will benefit. Talking about viral marketing is relevant here.

The disadvantage is that many of her friends' friends may not have dogs or may live outside Lottie's area. Also, many potential customers may not use social media. Lottie therefore needs to use other methods of promotion as well.

The disadvantages should be about the same length to give a balanced argument.

The conclusion should be relevant to the case study and the points you have made.

# Answers

The following pages contain answers to the 'Now try this' questions in Unit 2 of the Revision Guide.

## Learning aim A

### 1. Start-up costs

Any two of the following: builder's fees; decoration; furniture and fittings; catering equipment; installation of heating and lighting; advertising.

### 2. Operating (running) costs

Any two of the following: electricity; gas; fuel costs to deliver cakes; cake stands/boxes; ingredients for cakes; cake decorations.

### 3. Fixed and variable costs

(a) Any one of the following: rent; business rates; utility bills; insurance.

(b) Any one of the following: wood; paint; glue; screws; packaging.

### 4. Calculating total costs

1 £180          2 £300

### 5. Sources of revenue

B Selling clothes     C Donations from the public

### 6. Calculating revenue

Books: 1,200 × 0.25 = £300; DVDs: 500 × 0.20 = £100; Total = £400

### 7. Types of expenditure

A Rent £1000          D Wages £1,400

### 8. Understanding and calculating profit or loss

Profit = **Revenue − Expenditure**

## Learning aim B

### 9. Break-even charts

A The total costs line on a break-even chart represents fixed costs + **variable costs**.

B Where the total costs line crosses the total revenue line, this shows **the breakeven point**.

### 10. Interpreting break-even charts

1 100 toy boxes     2 £16,000          3 £80

### 11. Using the breakeven formula to calculate the break-even point

1 400 bikes          2 300 bikes          3 600 bikes

### 12. The value of breakeven analysis and the risks of ignoring it

Your answer should include some of the following points:
A breakeven analysis will help Salma plan a successful business as:

- She will have to identify the fixed and variable costs involved in developing the app and decide an appropriate selling price.
- She will need to forecast future sales.
- Then she will calculate her break-even point. If this is too high to achieve then she will have to try to reduce her costs or increase her price.
- Carrying out a breakeven analysis will show her whether it is worthwhile producing the app or whether the costs would be too high.
- If she did not do a breakeven analysis she would not know how many apps she would have to sell to make a profit and could lose money.

### 13. The effect of changes on the break-even point

1 The increase in costs will change the break-even point. It will go higher. The restaurant will have to sell more meals to break even.

2 Increasing the selling price will make the break-even point fall. This could compensate for the rise in costs.

3 The risk with Sally's idea is that fewer customers will visit the restaurant if prices increase.

### 14. The purpose of budgeting

The purpose of budgeting is to first identify expenditure and revenue. Expenditure levels are then set lower than revenue. This is essential for the business to make a profit. Kim will benefit because she will identify all her expenditure and potential revenue. She will have to reduce her forecast expenditure if this is too high to ensure that she makes a profit.

### 15. Budgeting and budgetary control

Budgetary control means checking that spending and revenue targets are met. This is important to ensure that Sye makes a profit. If he does not control his budget, he will not know if his costs are rising or if sales are too low. If he overspends then he could go out of business.

### 16. Cash flow forecasting

A Telephone bill

C Staff wages

### 17. Calculating net inflows/outflows

B (£2,000)

### 18. Impact of timings on cash flow

Any two answers from the following. Jack could:

- phone the customer and chase up the money and/or find out when he could be paid
- offer a small discount for immediate settlement
- ask for part payment
- reduce his expenditure as much as possible for that month, such as by delaying payments to his own suppliers
- ask the bank for a temporary overdraft
- defer any major expense items until he receives payment.

### 19. The benefits of using a cash flow forecast and the risks of not doing it

Jerome is putting his business at risk because all businesses need to forecast cash flow otherwise they may not have enough cash to pay their own bills. If Jerome's business was quiet for a few weeks or if he had a large emergency bill (for example, a repair bill for his van if it breaks down) then he could struggle. Unless he has allowed for this expenditure he would have to take out a loan or overdraft to pay for it or stop trading temporarily. Identifying his inflows and outflows will help him to plan to be successful.

### 20. Completing and analysing cash flow forecasts

1

|  | May (£) | June (£) | July (£) |
|---|---|---|---|
| Total receipts | 14,000 | 8,000 | 9,000 |
| Total payments | 5,500 | 12,000 | 7,500 |
| Net inflow/outflow | 8,500 | (4,000) | 1,500 |
| Opening balance | (1,000) | 7,500 | 3,500 |
| Closing balance | 7,500 | 3,500 | 5,000 |

2 It is a good time for Megan to plan to expand because she has spare cash available to pay for the work.

## Learning aim C

### 21. Cost of sales

1  Cost of sales means the money it costs to make a product.

2  **A** Flowers     **B** Ribbon

3  She needs to know her cost of sales so that she can deduct this amount from her sales revenue to calculate her gross profit.

### 22. Gross profit

Plants £45,000 + sheds £55,000 = total gross profit £100,000

### 23. The impact of positive and negative gross profit

1  Positive gross profit is important because it is essential to the survival of the business.
(Any of the following)

- It is needed to pay the expenses and to provide money to invest in better equipment or expansion.
- It also tells the owner that the cost of sales is not too high and that the business can do well if sales volumes remain high.

2  If Tariq makes a negative gross profit then he:

- has to look at lowering his cost of sales, which are too high
- should also try to increase his sales revenue by selling more goods.

### 24. Net profit

- Gross profit is the amount remaining when the cost of sales is deducted from sales revenue.
- Net profit is the amount left when all the business expenditure has been deducted from the gross profit figure.

### 25. The impact of positive and negative net profit

1  Oliver's net profit is lower than his gross profit because he has deducted his business expenditure from his gross profit figure.

2  Oliver must reduce his business expenditure which is £18,000.

### 26. Financial statements

1  Income statement (profit and loss account) and statement of financial position (balance sheet).

2  • The bank will want to check that Paula is making a positive gross and net profit.

- They will want to see her assets and liabilities to see what she owns and what debts she has.

### 27. Income statement (profit and loss account)

|  | £ | £ |
| --- | --- | --- |
| Income from sales |  | 28,000 |
| Cost of sales | 8,000 |  |
| Gross profit |  | 20,000 |
| Expenses |  |  |
| Utilities | 4,000 |  |
| Car expenses | 2,400 |  |
| Net profit |  | 13,600 |

### 28. Assets, liabilities and working capital

**A**  • Fixed assets are items the business will always need to have to be able to operate, such as a motor vehicle or a computer.

- Current assets are cash or items that are easily converted to cash, such as stock, or assets that are used to pay short-term debts (current liabilities).

**B**  • Trade receivables are an asset because they are customers who owe money to the business.

- Trade payables are a liability because they are people the business must pay, such as suppliers.

### 29. The statement of financial position (balance sheet)

1  Mo's current assets are the £5,000 he has in the bank and his owed revenue of £300. His current liabilities are his overdraft of £200 and the £800 he owes suppliers.

2  Mo's van is a fixed asset so is not part of the calculation to find working capital. His current assets of £5,300 − current liabilities £1,000 = working capital £4,300.

### 30. Completing a statement of financial position (balance sheet)

| ASSETS | £ | £ |
| --- | --- | --- |
| **Fixed assets** |  |  |
| Equipment |  | 750 |
| Van |  | 1,500 |
| **Current assets** |  |  |
| Stock | 3,000 |  |
| Trade receivables | 200 |  |
| Cash in bank | 500 | 3,700 |
| **Total assets** |  | 5,950 |
| LIABILITIES |  |  |
| **Current liabilities** |  |  |
| Trade payables | 600 |  |
| Overdraft | 350 | 950 |
| **Working capital** (Net current assets) |  | 2,750 |
| **Total assets less current liabilities** |  | 5,000 |
| **Shareholders' funds** |  |  |
| Share capital | 5,000 |  |

### 31. Increasing profits and analysing an income statement (profit and loss account)

- Asiya should focus on reducing her cost of sales by trying to negotiate cheaper supplies with her existing suppliers. She could also look at using different suppliers or trying to substitute some of the materials she uses for cheaper items, providing this will not spoil the quality. This will increase her gross profit.
- She should also try to reduce her gas bill. She could change supplier or look to see if there are ways she can make savings and use less gas. She could also change to electric heating instead of gas.

### 32. Analysing a statement of financial position (balance sheet) for a small business

Marianne owes £4,500 to her suppliers and has a fairly large overdraft. If she raises money by selling stock and getting money in from her trade receivables then she should lower the amount she owes by paying these bills. She should also pay off some of her overdraft if possible because she will be paying bank charges on this. However, she needs to keep a check on her working capital. At the moment it is too low.

The following pages contain answers to the 'Now try this' questions in Unit 9 of the Revision Guide.

## Learning aim A

### 36. Defining marketing and its importance to business

Marketing involves identifying the needs, wants and expectations of current and potential customers and providing goods and services that meet these needs profitably.

### 37. How businesses use marketing

Any two of the following:

- Understanding customer needs: the business needs to understand the difference between the needs of customers in the UK and in the new markets so that products can be adapted accordingly.
- Communication: the business will need to communicate with the public in the new markets and will have to find the best way of doing this.
- Differentiation: the business needs to ensure that it understands the products made by competitors and can try to ensure that its own is different in some way.
- Benefits to customers: the business will need to increase sales by ensuring that customers gain a specific benefit from choosing the UK product.

### 38. Marketing, corporate objectives and SMART objectives

The objective Jen has written is not time-based. She should add a time period, for example to increase sales by 5 per cent over the next six months or over the next year.

### 39. B2B and B2C markets

Any two of the following:

- His prices will have to be competitive as the care homes will likely want to pay monthly after receiving an invoice.
- He will have to deliver the fruit and vegetables.
- He will be expected to provide large quantities on specific dates.
- They may ask him to choose the best fruit and vegetables for the season and deliver them at a fixed price.

### 40. Other types of markets

Capital goods are goods bought by businesses or industry to help them make other products or provide their service.

### 41. Business models

A  The sales model – goods are presented at a bargain price; customers choose whether to buy or not.

B  The advertising model – the blogger earns money through related advertising.

C  The marketing model – the landscape gardener will tailor each garden to his client's needs and the climate.

### 42. Business orientation and choice of business model

(a) BuzzAir originally had a product-orientated business and a sales model.

(b) By listening to feedback it is now more market orientated, it has developed a marketing model to attract and retain passengers and hopes to get repeat bookings.

### 43. Branding – its importance and dimensions

Any two of the following:

- Mark could use colours in the pub decorations and in his menus that reflect freshness, such as green and yellow.
- He could include illustrations in the pub to show how his food is sourced from local farmers and other suppliers.
- He could ask well-known local celebrities to visit and endorse the pub to gain publicity and attract customers.

### 44. The benefits of building brands

The brand is worth money. So if someone wanted to buy that brand to make further games they would have to pay a lot of money for it.

## Learning aim B

### 45. Market research – types and sources of data

(a) It will provide primary, qualitative data because Healthy-care will obtain customer opinions.

(b) Healthy-care can find out which products customers like and which they don't and what features they like and don't like, which will enable them to review their product ranges and drop unpopular items. They can also stock products that customers want to buy but currently can't find in their stores. They can also review any services that customers are not happy about and change these.

### 46. The uses of data to support marketing activity

(a) Qualitative data: she could ask her customers if they would be interested in a late-night opening or if they have friends who would be.
Quantitative data: she should look at how many clients she has every Monday and how much she earns that day and compare it with the other days she is open.

(b) She may discover that many of her customers work late so this trend would help her to make a decision. She may find that no other local hairdressers is open later at nights. This would show a gap in the market for a service that no one else provides.

### 47. The uses of internal and external data and situational analysis

Any two of the following:

- He will not know whether there is room in the market for two more fitness clubs or whether there are already established clubs in the other towns that could be strong competitors.
- He will not know if the lifestyle trend for fitness is increasing or decreasing.
- He will not be able to analyse which towns are the best locations, namely, where there is a gap in the market.
- He will not know about any of the threats that might jeopardise his future plans and mean that he loses money.
- He will not understand what has made his current club successful and how he could improve this to make it even better.

### 48. The purpose of market research and analysis

(a) Any two of the following:

- He could observe customers buying sports cars.
- He could read published reports on customers buying sports cars.
- He could act as a mystery shopper.
- He could set up a focus group of sports car owners and ask their opinions.
- He could devise a survey for sports car owners.

**(b)** It will enable Martin to offer products with features that his customers like. This means that the products will be more attractive and desirable to potential customers. He can also promote the products to attract customers' attention and he will know what to say to customers to encourage them to buy.

### 49. Interpreting key market research findings

In your evaluation, you should have:

- identified some positive points, including:
  - The bicycle market is large and estimated to grow until at least 2016.
  - More men cycle than women so this would indicate that there will be a demand for cycling clothes for men.
- suggested some negative points, for example:
  - A shop which only caters for men will miss out on sales to women who do also cycle – even if not in the same numbers as men.
  - Women's increased participation in cycling may be a key factor in the fact that the market is growing.
  - Sales may depend on where Joel lives and whether there will be a demand for expensive clothes in that area.
- concluded that he may be better off selling clothes for both men and women, or cheaper items, unless he can open his shop in an area which would attract male cyclists who want to buy designer clothing.

### 50. PESTLE analysis

Arguments for:

- The PESTLE analysis shows that people have more money to spend and the government wants to promote cycling and open more cycle lanes. This should help to increase demand.
- New technology also means that faster racing bikes are available and this will tempt racing enthusiasts to buy a new bike.

Arguments against:

- Making helmets compulsory may mean some people stop cycling.
- Selling racing bikes means he is not catering for ordinary families who want to purchase bikes to start cycling.

Conclusion:

- Racing bikes are a niche market and small businesses are often better focusing on a niche market where there is less competition and specialist products can be sold at a premium price.
- He would have less competition from large firms and could make a success of this if he is an expert and knows his product well.

### Learning aim C

### 51. The marketing mix – an overview

Place is important because customers need to be able to access products to buy them. Place affects whether or not the business is going to get high sales. Products need to be available in the right place at the right time or customers will be disappointed and probably buy an alternative item instead.

### 52. Product differentiation

The enhanced grip on the baby suits makes them different and more appealing. It is the USP and will set the product apart from its competitors. This should promote sales.

### 53. Product life cycle

1 The growth stage.

2 In the maturity stage, sales have peaked and sales growth will have slowed down. Launching a new product will be expensive and using extension strategies, such as changing the design or adapting the product in some way, may be a cheaper option. This will encourage sales from new and existing customers and the business may benefit from increased sales revenue.

### 54. Product portfolios

Customers have an image of a brand and the products it makes that appeals to them. A product which does not fit the image and focus of the business will confuse customers and may even be detrimental to the brand as a whole.

### 55. Pricing strategies

The DIY store is using competitive pricing because it wants to attract customers away from its competitors. The Italian tiles are set at a premium price because they are a desirable product. The plumber is using cost plus pricing because he has worked out how long the job will take and wants to cover his costs for the week and make a profit, which is his wage.

### 56. Elasticity of demand

Ken should lower the price of envelopes so that demand for these will increase again. He could increase the price of paper even more without losing many sales because demand for this is relatively inelastic.

### 57. Place – distribution channels

The three distribution channels are: selling online direct to customers; selling door to door to customers through representatives and selling through two retail stores.

### 58. Place – business location

Sales are likely to fall because there will be less passing trade. An ideal place for a jeweller is near to other jewellers so anyone looking for jewellery can compare what is in different shops. If there are other jewellers on the side street then this will help sales to stay the same because potential customers will still visit the area, but if the side street is very quiet, or if there is no parking nearby, then the jeweller is likely to see a fall in sales.

### 59. The promotional mix, budget and channels

Any two of the following.

A business could:

- include a discount voucher or a coupon in the magazine that customers have to return. It could then check how many vouchers/coupons have been returned
- include an offer that customers can only receive if they register on the website and then see how many website registrations it receives
- offer a product at a reduced price for a limited time and assess how many it sells
- advertise a special event and see how many people attend.

### 60. Viral marketing and guerrilla advertising

Guerrilla advertising means doing something different that will get attention and be noticed. People will then forward it to their friends using social media. One idea would be to use a flash mob with people dressed as hearts doing exercises. It could be filmed and posted on YouTube. Alternatively, Mark could ask people to come for a midnight run, using the app. He could use street art – for example, by painting a huge chalk heart with a pair of legs on the pavement, with the name of his app written beneath it.

## 61. Consistency and the marketing mix

Stylewise's target customers are young, fashion-conscious men and women who want a good range of clothes at cheap prices. There is a wide range of basic items available and prices are among the cheapest on the high street. Stores are all on busy streets or in shopping areas to maximise passing trade.

## 62. Ebusiness and ecommerce

Any two of the following:

- Customers will be able to see when items are out of stock so won't order these items and then be disappointed when they don't arrive.
- The business will know which items need restocking. Customers could be offered alternatives which they might then buy.
- Customers could be given the opportunity to be notified by email when the items are restocked.
- The business will know which items are fast sellers and may increase these stocks to prevent customers being disappointed.

## 63. Influences on the marketing mix

Two key influences on Techsmart's marketing mix are:

- changes in technology – it wants to be market leader
- cultural issues – specifically the buying behaviour of customers in developing nations who want cheaper products.

It has therefore introduced the fingerprint ID system to stay ahead of its rivals technologically and it has introduced cheaper phones so it has a wider range of price options for customers.

## 64. Evaluating the effectiveness of the marketing mix

SMART objectives are specific, measurable, achievable, realistic and time-based. If a SMART objective/target is not met there are likely to be issues with one or more elements of the marketing mix so the marketing mix needs to be reviewed. Questions should be asked about each of the 4 Ps – Product, Price, Place and Promotion – to see how these can be improved and how the marketing mix can be made more effective.

# Your own notes

# Your own notes

# Your own notes

# Revision is more than just this Guide!

## You'll need plenty of practice on each topic you revise

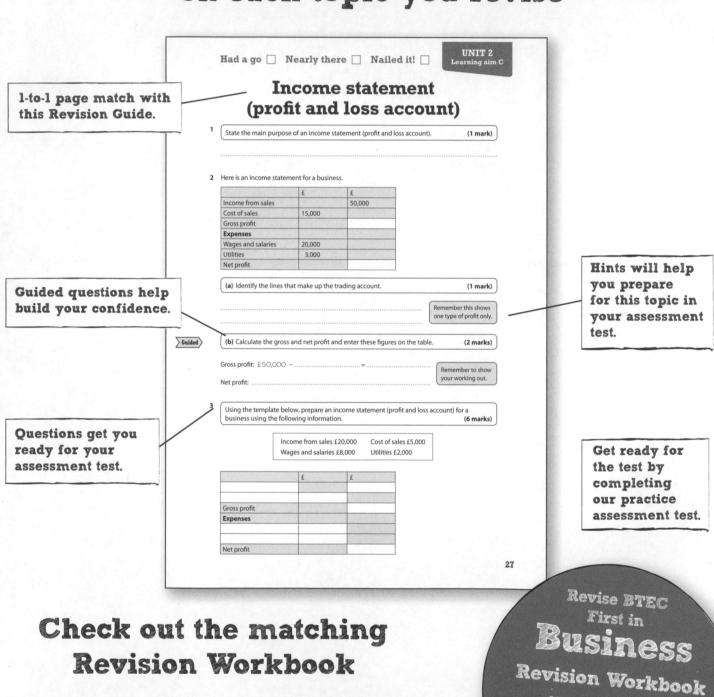

1-to-1 page match with this Revision Guide.

Guided questions help build your confidence.

Questions get you ready for your assessment test.

Hints will help you prepare for this topic in your assessment test.

Get ready for the test by completing our practice assessment test.

Had a go ☐   Nearly there ☐   Nailed it! ☐

**UNIT 2** Learning aim C

### Income statement (profit and loss account)

1  State the main purpose of an income statement (profit and loss account).   **(1 mark)**

2  Here is an income statement for a business.

|  | £ | £ |
| --- | --- | --- |
| Income from sales |  | 50,000 |
| Cost of sales | 15,000 |  |
| Gross profit |  |  |
| **Expenses** |  |  |
| Wages and salaries | 20,000 |  |
| Utilities | 3,000 |  |
| Net profit |  |  |

(a) Identify the lines that make up the trading account.   **(1 mark)**

Remember this shows one type of profit only.

**Guided**  (b) Calculate the gross and net profit and enter these figures on the table.   **(2 marks)**

Gross profit: £50,000 − ........................ = ........................

Net profit: ........................

Remember to show your working out.

3  Using the template below, prepare an income statement (profit and loss account) for a business using the following information.   **(6 marks)**

Income from sales £20,000   Cost of sales £5,000
Wages and salaries £8,000   Utilities £2,000

|  | £ | £ |
| --- | --- | --- |
|  |  |  |
|  |  |  |
| Gross profit |  |  |
| **Expenses** |  |  |
|  |  |  |
|  |  |  |
| Net profit |  |  |

27

## Check out the matching Revision Workbook

**THE REVISE BTEC SERIES FROM PEARSON**

www.pearsonschools.co.uk/revise

Revise BTEC First in **Business** Revision Workbook
978 1 4469 0669 9
UK Schools and Colleges price:
Just £2.49
RRP £3.99